THE THIRD GRADE READER

12 SHORT STORIES FOR KIDS IN 3RD GRADE

Curious Bee

CONTENTS

ATTENTION:

DO YOU WANT MY FUTURE BOOKS AT HEAVY DISCOUNTS AND EVEN FOR FREE?

HEAD OVER TO WWW.SECRETREADS.COM AND JOIN MY SECRET BOOK CLUB!

INTRODUCTION

If you are young, curious, and interested in animals, time travel, superheroes, technology, lemonade, or solving mysteries, then this book is for YOU! In these pages, you will enter the exciting worlds of people like yourself, who travel to the beach, through time, and anywhere that clues take them to solve the crime. Smart, strong, adventurous kids - along with their pets, lunch boxes, and imaginations – all have stories to tell and places to go!

Has your family ever gone on a road trip? I bet it didn't end up like this one!

What is it like to run a farm - take care of animals, drive tractors, and work at the fresh food stand? What do you expect at the beach? Swimming, sunshine, sand, sure. But what about a famous new musician filming the video for his newest song?

There are twists and turns where you least expect them in these 12 stories. Some focus on a kid just like you who goes on an exciting trip or adventure with friends.

There's even a story from the point of view of our pets - and what they do, say, and think when we are not around. And, how do babysitters handle a tough evening?

In this book, you will meet a real-life child hero named Ruby Bridges, who stood up for all kids in 1960. Could you be so brave? Have you ever lost your lunch box and wondered how it feels when it ends up in the Lost and Found?

If an eight-year-old took over a dairy farm, would it fall apart? Or would adults wish the eight-year-old could run the farm every day?

You will find all these answers and much, much more inside the pages of this book. Crime solvers, basketball players, lemonade sippers…. They are all waiting to meet you! Take a break from the real world of homework and chores. Get lost in this book that is full of adventure and fun, waiting for you to join in!

Which story will be your favorite?

A DAY IN THE LIFE OF PETS

Glub. Glub. Glub.

Tick. Tick. Tick.

ZZZ...ZZZ...ZZZ...ZZZ...ZZZ...

BUZZ! BUZZ! BUZZ! BUZZ! BUZZ!

Henry brought his palm down hard on his alarm clock, stopping it mid-buzz. He yawned loudly and tried to feel a bit more awake. Henry had been dreaming about the playground, climbing on the rope ladder, and sliding down the loopy slide. He could still feel the sun on his face as he wandered over to his fish bowl. Goldie, the tiniest, cutest goldfish from the pet shop, made lazy left turns around the bowl. Henry stared. *How did Goldie not go crazy from boredom?* He wondered.

Goldie stared back at Henry. Glub, glub, good morning, Henry..., left turn..., hey, where did you go? Glub, glub..., left turn..., oh, there you are..., Goldie thought to himself.

Food! Glub! Food! Goldie thought and swam upward toward his flakes. He slowed before slamming into his breakfast and sucking it into his mouth.

Yum, same as yesterday! I am one lucky little fish. He ate four more flakes as Henry left the room, but then he came back and approached Goldie's bowl again.

"It's going to be a great day, Goldie!" Henry told the little fish. "If I could, I would high-five you!"

Left turn..., where is Henry..., left turn..., oh, there is Henry..., left turn..., where is Henry...?

Henry bounded out of his room and down the steps to the kitchen, barely missing Kala, the cat. She was in her usual spot; the family had named it "Kala's Step," and it was the third from the bottom. Her black and gray fur was dotted with white on her belly and ears, and she purred constantly.

Henry skipped over Kala expertly and rounded the corner into the kitchen. His dad had breakfast ready for him, eggs and bacon and a glass of orange juice, which was the same every day.

"Good morning, Dad!" Henry said as he plopped down and started eating.

His dad could tell he was excited. He knew Henry was hurrying to get to school because of the big class trip. Every spring, the third graders at North Fountain Elementary School went to the city zoo. There were pandas, giraffes, and elephants, and there was also an arcade.

Henry finished his breakfast and grabbed his jacket. There was a chill in the air, but he barely noticed as the door slammed shut behind him.

Kala was startled at the noise; she knew what that meant. Henry had left for the day, and she didn't have to pretend to be a sleepy lump on the third-to-bottom step anymore. The day could begin.

In the kitchen, Dad was cleaning the breakfast dishes. Kala quietly tiptoed down the steps and crept into the kitchen. *Yes, Henry's dad is almost finished cleaning up,* Kala thought. Dad always saved the pan for last, and there he was, rinsing away the soapy bubbles and reaching for the blue towels to dry it. Before he could notice her, Kala went to find Hoover.

Oh, Hoover. Hoover was a Boxer who had moved in with the family last year. He was not fully grown, yet not a puppy. Henry loved him, and Goldie, well, who could tell? Hoover loved adventure, which kept Kala from being bored. *So,* Kala thought to her feline self, *he is good for something.*

Kala found Hoover in his usual spot: on a big, yellow-and-green pillow in the living room, at the foot of the fireplace. The sun perfectly hit that spot in the early afternoon, and Hoover would take a long, dreamy nap.

This morning, though, Hoover opened one eye as soon as Kala appeared in the living room doorway and gave her a doggie smile.

"Don't get too excited," she cautioned, "but Henry just left for school."

Hoover immediately stood up and wagged his tail. He knew what came next. When Dad finished cleaning the kitchen, he would grab his keys and go to work. The three pets would be alone.

While other pets might pace all day restlessly, waiting for their people to return, Hoover, Kala, and Goldie had other plans.

Kala turned and walked back to the kitchen. She quickly jumped onto the counter and turned on the sink. She adjusted the temperature and opened a low-hanging cabinet with her front paw. The box of plastic bags was up front, and Kala snagged one quickly in her teeth. She held the bag under the running water. Goldie was so small and cute; she didn't need much water and could fit easily into a Ziplock baggie. Hoover trotted to the kitchen counter, took the bag of water in his teeth from Kala, and carefully climbed the steps to Henry's bedroom.

Goldie was still swimming in lazy left turns. It took three laps before he noticed Hoover.

"Hoover!" Goldie said. "Nice to see you again. Is it time?"

Hoover stared at the little fish with a water bag hanging from his mouth. It was apparent to Hoover the time had come for the three pets to start their adventure!

Goldie knew that this was the start of their daily routine. The three pets waited for the humans to leave each morning, taking turns planning their day.

Today was Kala's day, and she knew what she wanted to do and where she wanted to go. Hoover needed to get Goldie settled in his water bag, and they could be on their way.

A few minutes later, Hoover returned downstairs with Goldie hanging from the buckle of Hoover's collar, still making lazy left turns around the plastic baggie.

Kala gave them both a knowing look and smiled, "let's go."

They walked through the kitchen to the porch door. Kala knew just how to jump from the counter to catch the door handle, so it unlocked and clicked open at the same time. After they moved through, Hoover kicked it closed with one swift move.

"Where to, boss?" Hoover looked over at Kala, who was sniffing at the air.

"Left," she said and started walking. Kala lowered her head and ears and moved around to the front of the house. The friends hiked along the sidewalk until they reached the big intersection, where streets crossed each other and cars drove quickly. They knew to be careful here. Hoover stepped out in front, the oldest and strongest, to protect his little friends.

When the cars and buses stopped whizzing past, Hoover nodded at Kala, and they crossed the street. In just a few more steps, they arrived at their first destination - Mrs. Harte's house.

Mrs. Harte lived in a small, white house with blue shutters on the corner. Her windows were always open, and her television was always on. She lived with her cat Melon, a gray longhair she adopted many years ago, who sat on her lap while she napped on the couch. Melon was content to lounge around Mrs. Harte's house all day. Although, he loved visitors - especially Kala, Hoover, and Goldie.

Kala could hear the sounds of Mrs. Harte's television as she strolled up the driveway. As usual, the front windows were open despite the chill in the air. Kala quickly jumped up and landed gracefully on the windowsill. Melon was purring softly on Mrs. Harte's lap while a man on the television talked and talked. Kala could not understand how Mrs. Harte watched this on TV all day. *Maybe*, Kala thought to herself, *that's why she naps so much.*

Melon looked up then, and his tail shot straight into the air. He hopped off Mrs. Harte's lap and put his paws on the windowsill next to Kala, and she bent down to touch noses with him.

"Heeeeeeey," Melon said. "I didn't know you were coming today! Can I offer you a drink?"

Kala jumped into Melon's living room. Melon put his paws down and walked over to his water bowl, and he nudged it closer to Kala with his nose.

Hoover stuck his head into the room through the window.

Melon looked up. "More friends! Come in! Come in!"

Hoover jumped through the window but with less grace than Kala, but he and Goldie landed safely. Goldie kept swimming his lazy laps, and Kala wondered for a moment why they had brought him along. *Well,* she thought, *he deserves a day out, too, I guess.*

Hoover strolled over to the couch. He found the small black rectangle with the numbers on it. Kala knew he was not very smart, but he knew how to find the Animal Network on the TV, and he was the only one strong enough to push the buttons. Goldie swayed gently in his bag as Hoover walked.

With one quick push, the Animal Network sprang to life on the television. Kala's eyes grew large.

Fashion Pets.

She knew *Fashion Pets* would be on right now, which was on every morning. *Fashion Pets* was the whole reason to visit Melon; watching *Fashion Pets* with Melon was Kala's favorite pastime. The two cats sat side by side on the floor in front of the television. Their tails touched gently while they watched the animals dressed in different outfits. Neither one of them could keep track of what animals were wearing. Dogs as race car drivers. Bunnies as ballerinas. Cats as firefighters. Even animals dressed up as different animals. Humans spoke in the background, but Kala and Melon weren't listening. Their furry little heads turned left and right as the animals ran, hopped, and jumped.

Behind them, Hoover yawned. He thought *Fashion Pets* was OK, but how long would they sit there and watch animals playing dress-up on TV? He looked over at Mrs. Harte. She was still sleeping, snoring softly, and she had no idea visitors were here. Hoover wandered over to her and sat by her side.

"Goldie, can you see the TV?" he asked his fish friend.

"Yes…" Lazy left turn. "No…" Lazy left turn. "Yes…" Lazy left turn. "No…"

Kala could sense Hoover's restlessness. She nuzzled her friend and enjoyed a few more moments of animals on the television. Then she stood, turned, and jumped onto the windowsill. Hoover pushed the button, so the TV showed the talking human again.

Kala felt her tummy rumble and knew Hoover must be hungry, too. Together the friends trotted across the street and made a left toward the town center. A delicious restaurant stood open for the day. Kala and Hoover knew the chefs were hard at work, and the scents of cooking food made their mouths water.

Goldie simply continued to swim in a circle in his bag.

Hoover spotted a back door left open just a crack. He stuck his nose inside and nudged it open. The door let out a low creak, but no one heard it over the sounds of chefs starting their day. Burgers had just been tossed onto the grill and were making a sizzling sound - and they smelled oh-so-good.

Kala and Hoover looked at each other knowingly. They both wanted a burger.

They waited patiently until the chef walked away, wiping her hands on her apron, and took a quick phone call. Then they moved into action.

Hoover swiped a spatula off the nearest counter and held it between his teeth. With one quick motion, he swept three burgers off the grill and onto the floor. Each grabbed a burger and moved swiftly toward the door as the chef ended her call and walked back to the grill.

"What? Where did those burgers go?"

Those were the last words Hoover and Kala heard as they stepped outside to enjoy their snack. They smiled to themselves as they wandered behind the restaurant, past the green dumpster. No one would see them here. Then they dropped their burgers and started eating. The burgers were fresh, hot, and delicious.

Kala was licking her lips, full and satisfied when Goldie spoke up.

"I wonder how Henry is doing."

Kala and Hoover looked at each other. As much fun as they were having on their day out, they missed Henry. He took excellent care of them: Henry walked Hoover, fed Goldie, and never stepped on Kala.

They stopped eating, and Hoover let out a whine. Kala stopped purring. For a moment, they sat in silence, feeling homesick and sad. Together the friends started for home. Back at the busy street, Hoover led them across once the cars stopped. They trudged down the sidewalk, yearning for their home.

The walk home seemed farther than the walk this morning. The chill in the air seemed stronger. Suddenly it felt much later. The sun was lower in the sky, and the shadows were longer

Kala leapt to knock the patio door handle open and led Hoover inside. She latched the patio door once her friends were safely inside and walked over to the stairs.

Hoover took Goldie to Henry's room, opened the bag with his teeth, and watched Goldie jump expertly back into his bowl.

"Thank you, Hoover," Goldie said, starting his lazy left turns in his bowl. "I had fun and am glad to be home."

Hoover nodded and walked out of the room. He could hear Kala settling herself in her spot…, the third to bottom step. It creaked just as she lay down. He stood at the top of the stairs and could see Kala. He was amazed by how she could find a spot, lay down, and rest. Amazing, Hoover thought. Kala is simply excellent.

Suddenly, Kala jumped to her feet. Hoover looked around, hearing nothing. What made Kala jump?

Then, Hoover saw him, too.

Henry! Henry was home!

Hoover bounded down the steps happily, barking. He put his paws up on the front door to greet Henry. Not to be outdone, Kala paced back and forth behind him, her eyes locked on the doorknob.

The doorknob turned.

Henry walked in, full of smiles and stories about the zoo and the arcade. He had won a small bouncy ball for his friends to play with, and within seconds Kala was swatting it all over the house. Hoover did not leave Henry's side and wasn't distracted by a toy won with tokens at the arcade.

He lived for Henry's cuddles and kisses, and Henry gave them out every day when he came home. Hoover drank it all in. He felt Henry's warmth as he hugged Hoover and scratched his head in that delightful spot between his ears. Hoover could sit with Henry all day and enjoy this.

Henry ran up the steps to his room, Hoover close on his heels. Kala heard them and scrambled to catch up. She found them in Henry's bedroom, looking at Goldie in his little glass bowl.

Left turn..., glub, glub, glub..., left turn..., glub, glub, glub....

"Hey, Goldie!" Henry said happily. "What a day I had!"

Henry told them about the exotic animals he'd seen, the bus ride with his friends, and the fun arcade games he played.

"...and then I turned in all my tickets for a bouncy ball for Hoover and Kala to play with!" He ended his story.

Henry looked slowly at each of his pet friends. He sighed.

"You poor creatures...," he said, "home all day while I had quite an adventure. What did you do today, I wonder?"

A DAY ON THE FARM

Carter groaned as the sun rose over the horizon, and the rooster called loudly. He thought about his chores: the cows, the chickens, and the farm stand. Carter thought about the long line of customers, holding lists and their money, in a rush to collect things and get home.

The Great Land Farm had been in Carter's family for over a hundred years. Something called a "century," his father was proud of saying. Great Land Farm was mainly a dairy farm, which meant it had dozens of cows that produced milk, and they made butter from the fresh milk to sell to people from the town. In addition to milk and butter, Carter's family sold homemade ice cream on the weekends.

Great Land Farms also had chickens. There was a large chicken coop on the south side of the property, where the chickens lived, ate, and walked in lazy circles while chasing each other and screaming. Well, maybe not yelling, but Carter didn't know how else to describe it. He hated the sound the chickens made.

Carter stumbled out of his bed and left it unmade. The blanket trailed after him and landed on the floor. Shivers ran up his spine as his feet touched the cool tiles in the bathroom, and his eyes burned when the light hit them.

Carter was not a morning person.

Outside the bathroom, he could hear his parents chirping away in the kitchen. The coffee pot was humming, the gas stove was making the familiar *tick-tick-tick* noise that came just before the flame ignited, and the sink dripped. Above it all, Carter heard his parents.

Jen and Dave Johnson, owners of Great Land Farms, were morning people.

They rose before the sun—even on Saturdays! Jen called herself the "Chicken Mama" and had a few t-shirts embroidered with the title. She fed the chickens, sang to them, named them, and cared for their every need. She collected their eggs and then transported them to the farm stand daily for sale.

Dave was the "Cow Guy," and he had matching t-shirts - "Great Land Farm Cow Guy," the shirt read. Dave was a black coffee kind of man, a solid and silent type who was laser-focused on a task. He worked hard and did not stop until the job was finished. And the job wasn't finished until it was done *right*.

Carter stumbled, still half asleep, from the bathroom to the kitchen. His robe hung off one shoulder, and his hair stood up in all directions. He had brushed his teeth but forgotten to wash his face. The glare from the sun streamed in through the kitchen windows, so he squinted them shut as best he could.

Jen and Dave exchanged looks. Dave put his coffee cup down and rolled his eyes.

"Goodness, Carter," he began, "you look dreadful."

Carter stood up straighter, hoping it would help. His father didn't notice.

Jen piped up, "honey, how about some breakfast? That will wake you right up!" She started getting a plate together, but Carter motioned to stop.

"I think I will just go back to bed," Carter said, "I am exhausted."

Jen and Dave looked at each other, more seriously now.

"You'll do what, now?" Jen said. "There's no going back to bed when there are farm chores."

Carter heaved a sigh and knew there was no winning this argument.

"What's on my list?" He asked.

"We thought we'd try something new today," Dave said, "your mother and I are going to head out to the north fields and see if they are ready for planting."

"But that could take all morning!" Carter protested. "Who will tend the chickens? Collect the eggs? Milk the cows? Open the farm stand?"

Jen smiled. "Carter, my beautiful boy, you're almost ten! That's double digits!"

"Oh, no!" Carter was fully awake now. "Not me! Are you crazy?!"

His father put a firm hand on Carter's shoulder. "You have watched Mom and me for years. You know what to do. Cows first, and then chickens. Then the store. We will be back at the house by dinner."

Carter watched as his parents put their dishes in the sink and walked out the front door. He heard the car engine start and saw it turn up the road that cut through their property and led to the planting fields.

Unbelievable, Carter thought. And then, aloud, he said - "I had better write this down."

Carter rummaged through the kitchen drawers and found a pen and a pad of paper. What had his father said? Chickens first or cows? *Think, Carter, think.*

Carter heard the cows growing restless in the pasture and remembered that they become uncomfortable if they need to be milked and aren't.

He wrote down on his paper:

#1: Milk the Cows

Underneath, Carter wrote:

#2: Deal with chickens

Finally, Carter wrote:

#3: Open store, sell things

Carter felt organized and ready to start his day - except for his pajamas. The cows grew louder, and through the window, he could see them moving towards the shed where they get milked. They knew the routine and would be annoyed if milking was late. So, Carter quickly found a t-shirt and denim overalls, trying as much as possible to look like Dad.

Carter ran across the front lawn to the cow shed. The smell of the cows was unexpected, and for a moment, he thought he might pass out. Standing there, he noticed every one of the cows in their stalls staring at him, probably wondering what his problem was.

Carter needed to prepare for the number of cows in the cowshed. There were five along each wall. A small stool sat near the entrance to the shed, and a silver bucket sat on a shelf next to each stall. Carter remembered that once a cow filled the pail with milk, the milk went into a machine in the back of the room for sterilization and bottling, and he was grateful for work he didn't have to do himself.

Let's get started, Carter thought, pulling the stool towards the back of the first cow. He sat uncomfortably and started milking the way his father had taught him. Milking a cow was not challenging work when the cow was cooperative. Luckily this first one was, and Carter took to calling her Bessie. He called all the cows Bessie. After milking each cow, he carried his heavy pail to the back of the shed and dumped the milk into the machine for bottling.

By cow number four, Carter's hands ached, and he was so bored he stopped paying attention to his work. Clumsily, he knocked over a full pail of milk and had to start over.

Working on cow number seven, Carter developed a wicked pain in his neck and took to rotating it constantly while milking. Moving his neck slowed him down considerably. But when he stopped, the pain was unbearable.

At cow nine, exhaustion took over. Carter leaned against Bessie's thigh and nodded off. His hands slid off her udder and splashed into a pail full of milk. It was a rude awakening.

Carter washed up in the sink near the machine in the back of the cowshed. *One more cow*, Carter thought to himself, *just one more.*

He approached her slowly and looked her in the eyes. "We are going to be friends, you and me," he told her. "I decided your name is Bessie. I am Carter. Let's get this over with." He moved the stool into position and grabbed the pail. He rolled his shoulders to loosen up and tried to give himself a pep talk. "You can do this, Carter," he said. "You can milk one more cow."

Then the sound began. It started as a low rumble at the far end of the cowshed. Then it seemed to move from one cow to the next. It grew in volume like a thunderstorm gliding closer and closer. When the wall of sound arrived at Carter's feet, it almost knocked him over.

The cows had begun mooing all at once, protesting Carter's presence. They had had enough and wanted Dave back.

Carter thought - *I was so silly to think they wouldn't know the difference between my dad and me. What now?*

Defeated, he moved on to the chicken coop.

The chickens lived in a red coop with a black roof that Mom had built on a small hill near the cowshed. About 20 chickens roamed around their small pen, picking at seeds, sipping water, or sitting on eggs in rows in the coop. They made a terrible racket as he approached, but Carter was determined to show his parents he could handle these chores. He had almost been successful with the cows. How difficult could a few chickens be?

As it turned out, chickens could be complicated. Chickens resting quietly in a coop did NOT like to be disturbed, though no one had bothered to tell Carter. When he merrily swung the door to the cage open and shouted, "Good morning, chickens!" They startled, screamed, and started flying around. As they flew, feathers went everywhere.

Carter's chickens had no sense of direction, so they flew into his face and head, landed in his hair, and sat on his feet. They riled each other up until Carter had no choice but to leave the coop without a single egg. Outside, a few chickens waited for feed; they came running at Carter.

"Argh!" Carter yelled and jumped backwards at the sight of charging chickens.

He tripped over the trough and sat squarely in the water, spraying it everywhere. The chickens retreated in fear. Carter stood up, but the damage was done: his overalls were ripped and soaked, and he was far away from home. He picked up the bucket of chicken feed again and sprinkled some all around, and the chickens slowly walked back towards him, pecking at the ground. Some even dared to come out of the coop, and Carter saw an opportunity.

He took his soggy self into the enclosure, slowly and quietly this time, put the feed pail down, and picked up the lined egg basket. Beautiful oval eggs remained in the spots chickens had left to go out to find the feed. Carter gingerly picked up ten of them, covered them with the egg blanket to keep them from breaking, and headed back to the house.

Droplets of water fell off Carter's overalls as he walked, and he could feel puddles forming in his shoes. He put the egg basket into the large refrigerator and went back inside to change.

Carter pulled a fresh t-shirt over his head and new denim jeans on his legs and threw his wet, dirty clothes from the morning into his hamper. They smelled terrible. He grabbed a handful of dry cereal and a glass of orange juice, and as he returned the carton to the refrigerator, he noticed the cars parked in front of his house.

Was it noon already?

Carter frantically checked the kitchen clock and breathed a sigh of relief. It was only 11:30. People lined up early for Great Land Farm products. He knew several families in town drove to the farm stand in the middle of their workday just to grab some fresh milk and eggs before they ran out. The cars reminded Carter…, he had better check the stock in the farm stand refrigerators.

Carter jogged across the field with the store key on his belt, unlocked the side entrance, and checked the refrigerators. There certainly needed to be more for an afternoon of customers. Mom and Dad had not left specific instructions.

What should I do? Carter thought. Then he remembered milk running through the bottling machine in the cowshed and the fresh eggs in the house.

Carter left the little farm stand, locking the door behind him. His first stop was the cowshed. The machine had just finished bottling. To Carter's amazement, his morning's milking had yielded about 70 gallons of milk! Freshly bottled and chilled, ready for the farm stand shelves. Carter transferred them by wheelbarrow, slowly and carefully.

When he finished stocking the milk neatly in rows, Carter returned to the chickens. He entered the coop quietly and slowly, as he had seen Mom do. Carter collected four dozen eggs - and hoped many more were waiting in the farm stand refrigerator.

People started getting out of their cars; Carter noticed and ambled toward the entrance of the farm stand. They formed a line and chatted, waiting for Carter to open. Carter's heart started to pound, and he missed his mom and dad. It was one thing to handle farm chores but quite another to come face to face with customers who expected Great Land Farm service.

Carter returned to the farmstand and unlocked the side entrance. He took his time loading the eggs into cartons; they needed special care. Carter could hear the din of conversation outside the front entrance, a red-and-white Dutch door. When Carter finished with the eggs, he unlocked the cash register and counted the money inside. Stalling for time, he neatened the tens, fives, and ones. Carter looked around. There was nothing left to do.

The clock struck noon. Carter froze.

The conversation outside stopped for a moment. Then came a gentle knock on the Dutch door.

"Hello in there?" Someone asked, "are you open today?"

Carter swallowed hard and walked over to the Dutch door. He unlatched the top half and swung it open slowly.

"Good afternoon, and welcome to Great Land Farm!" He said to the gentleman standing before him. Carter noticed how long the line was and winced. He hoped they all wanted a single egg.

"Well, young man, I didn't expect to see you here," the customer said, "where is the Cow Guy, or the Chicken Mama, hmm?"

"Those are my parents, sir," Carter answered honestly, "they left me to tend the farm today while they inspected some fields."

"You've been doing farm chores all morning by yourself?" The man took off his sunglasses, and his eyebrows shot up in surprise.

At that moment, Carter recognized this customer. This man had been visiting the farm for milk and eggs at least once a week ever since he could remember. He was older and had a polite way about him. He always wore a suit, no matter the temperature, a driving cap, and a pocket square in his jacket. He looked like a businessman - a gentleman.

"Well, yes, sir," Carter answered. "Not too well, but all morning, yes!"

"Not too well?" The well-dressed customer looked concerned. "How so?"

The line of people behind him was growing restless, with some "let's go!" and "come on!" and "hurry up!" tossed around.

Carter and his customer pretended not to hear. "I had some difficulty with the chickens..., and the cows..., and I lost track of time getting the farm stand open...," Carter gestured to the line and the grumpy customers.

"Pipe down!" The well-dressed man shouted behind him. "The kid's on his own today!"

Carter smiled.

His customer leaned closer. "I'd like a gallon of fresh milk and a dozen eggs. Keep the change." Then came the wink.

Carter's mouth dropped open. That was a huge tip!

"People around here seem to have forgotten the value of hard work," the customer said, loud enough for the rest of the line to hear. "Forgotten what it is like to appreciate the labor of others, especially those smaller and still learning how things run..., they've forgotten their patience, and they've forgotten their manners." He turned to lean in closer to Carter. "Not me, though. I've been coming here for years, and your parents are the best farmers around, with the freshest eggs and the silkiest milk. You take your time, kid. You'll get there."

With that, he put his sunglasses back on and looked away, across the fields and into the distance. Carter put his money into the cash register and gathered his order.

"Thank you," Carter's customer said while looking him right in the eye, "you keep doing what you're doing. Make your parents proud." He took his order, turned away, and returned to his car.

Carter felt encouraged. He handled the rest of the customers without one mistake, and his confidence grew.

Jen and Dave pulled up just as Carter handed the last customer her change.

"Thank you for visiting, and come again!" Carter told her cheerily.

Jen and Dave walked up to the farm stand and looked at the empty shelves and the full cash register. Then they looked at each other.

"Wow," Jen said, "I'm impressed!"

"Me, too!" Dave said, patting Carter hard on the shoulder. "How did you get it all done?"

Carter shrugged. "I'm still learning, but...can I do it again tomorrow?"

JUST A DAY AT THE BEACH

It started like any other beach day and ended when I danced in a Harry Harris video.

Dad loaded the trunk with so many beach items I thought it would never close. Picnic baskets. Yes, *multiple* baskets. A cooler filled with ice and drinks. There were towels and various bottles of sunscreen. I noticed the vast, brightly colored blanket on which the whole family could lie down. Dad always made sure wherever we went, we were prepared for anything.

Or so I thought.

Just a routine day at the beach, I thought, like all the other days on all the other summer Saturdays that came before this one. What does Dad think will go wrong?

Mom came striding out the door, looking like a movie star. She turned heads wherever she went. Mom wore her white floppy sunhat, and her sandals only reinforced the movie star look. And who wore lipstick to the beach?

Mom waved quickly at a neighbor cutting her lawn and called, "Hey, Marge, looking good!" before stopping at me and looking me up and down.

"Well, good morning to you, Devin," she said, "nice skirt. How about you tuck your tank top into it? That would make such a cute little outfit! Like a dancer in a video!"

I rolled my eyes but did it anyway. Mom flashed her famously beautiful smile at me and winked. I hated when Mom was right, and Mom was right all the time.

My older sister Rose was already in the car, and she had her earbuds in and was drowning out her reality again. This is how Rose handled a day out with the family - by pretending not to hear us. I figured she couldn't interact if she couldn't listen to us.

As we pulled away from the house, Rose looked out the window, mouthing the words to what I imagined to be a sorrowful song. The look on her face was twisted and tortured, which was how she'd been acting lately. *Teenagers.*

She couldn't be listening to my favorite musician, Harry Harris. His songs were upbeat, and always made me happy when I heard them. I asked Dad if he would put on any Harry Harris songs while he drove, but he said no, so I slouched down in my seat and tried to imagine what his music videos looked like in my head.

Dad drove onto the highway and picked up speed. I thought about why Rose could be sad. Didn't she like going to the beach? I did. I liked the salty air, the waves in the water, and the sun on my skin. Even if Mom lathered us from head to toe with sunscreen, I always managed to get a nice tan and a few freckles on my nose. From what I understand, most kids in third grade don't like freckles, but I liked mine. I liked it when the sun brought them out more.

I glanced at Rose again. Now her eyes were closed, and she was snoring quietly. *Teenagers.* Rose was always falling asleep.

Dad gazed back at me in the rearview mirror. "Devin," he started, "are we going to ride some big waves today?"

I said, "of course!" while smiling. Dad and I always swam far into the ocean, leaving Mom and Rose on shore. We loved diving and bobbing up and down with the tide.

We arrived at Betadale Beach a short time later. The four of us piled out of the car, and I noticed the parking lot was full of strange-looking vans and men and women wearing exceedingly UN-beach-ready clothes. I squinted at the equipment they all seemed to be carrying. *Cameras, microphones stands and instruments? What was happening here?*

Rose woke up when we parked and got out of our car. She noticed the activity, too.

"What's going on? Who are these people?" She asked as if she had just plopped down on Planet Earth. She took her earbuds out of her ears because, for once, she wanted to hear the answer. I knew she felt something important was happening, and I grew even more curious.

"I have no idea," I answered.

Dad asked us to start unloading the contents of the trunk into the pull-along wagon, so we did, watching the people unloading the various pieces of equipment.

Once everything was out of the trunk and into the wagon, Dad started pulling it across the sand. Unloading began, and it took a while. Rose and I kept looking over our shoulders. What was going on? We could see the group setting up what appeared to be a photo shoot on the beach, with the addition of movie cameras. Could it be a TV show? Or a movie scene?

Mom offered us cold water the moment everything was unpacked. Rose took one and then got into her bikini. I declined and stayed in my regular clothes.

"Devin," Dad said, "aren't you going to get your bathing suit on? I thought we were swimming?"

"It's on under my clothes, Dad," I answered him, "and I want to wait a few minutes. This looks interesting," I motioned to the now extensive group of people down the beach, setting up a shot or a scene. We still couldn't tell.

Mom tried to distract us.

"Oh, leave those poor people alone!" She said, "they are obviously working on something. Don't stare. Have some manners." With that, she lay back on the blanket and opened a magazine.

Rose guzzled her bottle of water. "Ugh," she said, "it is sooo hot!" She reached for another bottle, which was also finished instantly.

The family stared.

"What?" Rose said, with that annoyed tone. "Water is good for me!"

34

"The water is also for everyone here, my dear," Dad said, "slow down."

"Ugh," Rose rolled her eyes again and sat crossed-legged on the blanket. "Whatever. Where are my earbuds?" She rummaged through her bag for a few minutes.

"Sweetie, come here so I can put lotion on your back," Mom said. I was annoyed but did not roll my eyes. It was the same routine on every beach Saturday.

Rose still could not find her earbuds. "Where...are... THEY?!" She yelled and dumped her whole bag onto the blanket. She had her wallet, keys, cell phone, some wrinkled pieces of paper, gum, mints, and other indescribable things.

"Rose dear," Mom started, "maybe you left them in the car."

"Fine. I need the restroom anyway! All that water...," Rose seemed plenty annoyed, but Mom was usually right about these things.

Rose stormed off in a huff, grabbing her sandals as she fled the family banket. She was almost a blur. I watched her strut across the beach and back toward the direction of the car. She'd be gone a while. That's when I noticed the limousine.

A few men in suits surrounded the sleek black car. I stopped watching Rose and started watching the limo.

"How about we get ready for the water, kiddo?" Dad asked me, but I barely heard him. Something big was about to happen. I could feel it. Dad had no interest in the parking lot. He was already in his bathing suit, slathered with suntan lotion, and ready to hit the waves.

I waved at Dad to be quiet without taking my eyes off the car. Who was inside? What were they doing at the beach? What was about to happen?

Mom sat up, too. She shielded her eyes from the glaring sun and looked at the limo.

"Wow, that is quite a car!" She said, then, reading my mind, she added, "I wonder whose it is?"

And then it happened. One of the well-dressed gentlemen leaned across the backdoor and grabbed the handle. All the activity on the beach promptly stopped, and all eyes were on the opening door. I held my breath. This was exciting!

Harry Harris, the number one pop star, stepped out. He was wearing black leather pants and a long scarlet leather coat with a white collar. He had big sunglasses on, but there was no mistaking it; I could spot him across a football field. Harry Harris was on my beach!

"Isn't that Harry something or other?" Mom asked, looking at me. "The singer you like?"

"Uh-huh," I answered, feeling a little dizzy and faint. "Harry Harris, the singer I like."

"Didn't I just say that?" Mom laughed. "Devin, are you OK?" Mom asked me.

"Oh, uhmm, yeah, I think," I stammered back, still watching Harry Harris. He had made his way from his car to the center of the group. There was a tall chair set up for him, and people were working on his hair and putting makeup on his face.

"Walk over!" Mom said in her super confident voice. "Go see what's happening. Doesn't look like many people have noticed him yet. I'll go with you."

Mom was correct about that: no one else seemed to have noticed Harry. His people had set up on the back of the beach, and most people were facing the water. Once people realized he was there, he would be mobbed. I was just a kid, but this was a once-in-a-lifetime chance.

"I'll go with you," Mom repeated, standing.

"No!" I said quickly. I was going to do this like a grown-up. By myself! "I can handle this."

Mom and Dad looked at each other. Dad shrugged, and Mom looked at the distance between the family blanket and Harry's setup. It was a bit of a distance. I knew I could get there and back just fine, but my mom could be overprotective sometimes.

Mom sighed. "I guess it's OK. I can see you, and I will be watching," Mom relented.

I nodded happily, glad that Mom had given me the advice to tuck my tank top into my skirt before we left the house. She said I looked cute, and Mom knew fashion more than anything else.

I walked slowly, looking at all the equipment and motion surrounding Harry. I decided it must be a video shoot. This beach was certainly a beautiful location, and he had been on tour near our town. It did add up.

A tall, muscular man stepped in front of me as I walked closer to Harry's chair.

"Stop. This is a closed shoot. You can't get any closer."

"Oh, uh, sorry," I stammered. "But, uh," I glanced behind him, "is that Harry Harris?"

The man put his finger to his lips and raised his eyebrows. "We don't want everyone to know we are filming here, that's why we set up in the back. Are you a fan?"

I thought guards were usually mean, but this guy seemed cool.

"I am," I said. "I have all of Harry's albums."

"I see," said the guard. He held out his hand. "I'm Mike, Harry's personal bodyguard."

I shook Mike's hand. "I am Devin," I said. "I am ten years old. I'm here with my family, over there." I pointed to my mom and dad and realized Rose hadn't returned yet.

"Well, Ms. Devin," Mike said to me, "if you wait here, I will see if I can get you an autograph." Mike turned and walked away then, leaving footprints in the stretch of sand between them. He still had his shiny black shoes on with his dark suit, and I thought he must be very hot.

Mike walked to Harry's chair. Harry's hair and makeup people finished and walked away, and I could tell the two men were chatting about me. Mike pointed in my direction, and Harry looked over his shoulder at me.

I felt dizzy and almost passed out.

Mike walked back then, alone. He wasn't holding anything, so I knew I wasn't getting an autograph.

"Mr. Harris doesn't have a pen with him today," Mike said to me. I instantly felt disappointed. Mike saw my face drop. He added, "But he would like to know if you want to join him on set. Can you dance?"

"Yes, yes I can dance!" I replied happily.

"Let's go meet Mr. Harris," Mike said.

I followed Mike's footsteps to Harry Harris's chair, heart pounding. Harry stood up when I was near his chair, and he looked me right in the eyes and smiled.

"Harry, this is Devin. She is ten years old, and a big fan. She is here with her family." Mike pointed down the beach at Mom and Dad, and Rose who had recently returned to the blanket. She was standing and staring at them, and I could see her mouth hanging open. Rose knew what was happening. I bet she was regretting all those guzzled waters!

"Nice to meet you, Devin," Harry held out his hand for me to shake it, and the dizziness returned. Somehow my hand met his and he did all the shaking for both of us. "Can you dance? I need a couple of background dancers in my beach video."

I nodded weakly. "Yes," I started, "I can, uhmm, I can dance if you want me to."

Harry laughed. "OK then. If you dance in the background of my video today, I will find a pen from someone here - I mean, someone has got to have a pen here - and I will give you an autographed t-shirt. Is it a deal, Devin?"

He said my name!

"It's a deal," I replied, and we shook again.

That evening, my family and I were sitting around the dinner table. Rose had not said anything except, "I CAN NOT believe this!" For the entire afternoon. As for me, I planned on wearing my autographed Harry Harris t-shirt today, every day, and for the rest of my life.

GRANDMA AND RUBY

"Many adults do not believe a child can be a hero, but it is true."

This is how my grandmother started telling me about the day she met Ruby Bridges. We were sipping lemonade on her porch in New Orleans, Louisiana, on a hot July morning. Ice-cold lemonade, the homemade kind Grandma made those days, always felt good after breakfast. The air was hot and thick, and thunderstorms were rolling in. By the afternoon, Grandma and I wouldn't be out on the porch; we would be back inside her house, counting the seconds between lightning and thunder to see if the storm was getting closer or farther away.

I wanted Grandma to keep talking about a child hero. Grandma always had great stories. She grew up in New Orleans. Colorful, noisy, busy New Orleans. With so much happening, New Orleans always made a great backdrop for engaging stories.

"I met Ruby Bridges on a day just like today. It was cloudy. The air felt like..., like..., *something* important was about to happen. Something. But I didn't know quite what. No one did. I was only six years old, and if I hadn't brought that frog to school, I may never have known."

She giggled to herself. Her belly bounced a little when she giggled, and I knew that meant she was pleased. I leaned closer. She lowered her voice.

Grandma leaned forward and looked me right in the eyes. She put her lemonade down on the glass table between us.

"Do you want to hear about the day I met a child hero?"

The wind blew a little harder and clouds rolled by a little darker. I felt a chill despite the July heat. I almost dropped my lemonade.

"I sure do!" I answered.

Grandma leaned back in her rocking chair. She looked off into the distance, across the lake towards the road. A few wisps of grey and white hair escaped her bun and started blowing across her face in the breeze. Grandma expertly tucked the stray hair behind her ear and started talking.

"It all started with that darn frog." Grandma started talking.

"What frog?" I asked.

Grandma looked at me like I should know what she was talking about.

"The frog!" she repeated. "The frog that Mama said I couldn't bring to school!

Grandma went on to tell me that after breakfast that November morning, there was a frog on her front porch. She was so excited when it made the *ribbit* sound and jumped closer to her.

"That frog," she wiggled a long bony finger at me, "was jumping towards me! That frog *wanted* to be my pet!"

43

Then she shook her head and sighed.

"I had scooped up that poor little animal, marched right back into my house, and showed it to my Mama."

"What happened?" I was riveted.

Grandma smiled widely. "My mama screamed like mad and said, 'NO WAY! GET THAT THING OUT OF HERE!'"

"What did you do?" I asked, leaning in closer.

"Well, if I couldn't bring that frog into my house, it would certainly come to school with me! I put that frog into my dress pocket and started toward William Franz Elementary School. I was going to show my teachers and my friends, and I wanted it to become the class pet." Grandma stopped for a breath and a sip of cool lemonade. I did the same.

Then Grandma continued. "When the frog and I approached the school, many people were there. I couldn't even see my way in! I had named the frog 'Hopper' by then. Isn't that a great name for a frog?"

I knew she didn't expect an answer.

"I talked to Hopper all the way to school. I could tell Hopper did NOT like all the noise they were making. Yelling. Stomping. Holding signs. I was only six, and Hopper was a frog, so we didn't know what the signs said." Grandma looked over and winked at me with that last part.

"Grandma, I know frogs can't read."

"Of course, you do," she answered me. "The older kids who walked to school with me seemed to know what was happening but didn't want to tell me. One boy took my hand and walked me in a wide circle away from the crowd and into the building through a side door to the school. I didn't know what I was scared of, but I knew it was scary outside my school. Hopper had stayed low in my pocket, and I tell the truth now," she looked straight at me again, "this is an important part; I did not remember Hopper was in there!"

She paused for a moment and smiled. I wondered if I should believe her. Before I could ask, Grandma started talking again.

"As luck would have it, the minute I sat at my desk and started writing the date on a clean sheet of paper - it was November 14, 1960 - Hopper decided to jump out of my pocket. I was shocked! The class started to yell. Some girls stood on their chairs and pointed as the frog hopped around the room."

She took a lemonade sip. Her throat must have been dry from all the talking.

"I wondered why they were so scared. Frogs hop, you know?"

I nodded eagerly and sipped my lemonade. The clouds grew darker, and in the distance, I heard thunder begin.

"A boy named Mikey caught Hopper and gently brought him to me." Grandma continued. "I reached out for him, but the teacher walked over with the garbage can and insisted Mikey put him in. She covered the garbage can with a framed poster from the wall and asked Mikey to release the frog outside. I thought the ordeal was over." Another giggle. "Oh, Hopper."

"But Grandma, was Mikey the hero?"

"Oh no, honey, Mikey was definitely not the hero!" She replied. "Sometimes things get worse before they get better."

Thunderclap. There was a very loud thunderclap, and the sky grew even darker.

"After Mikey took Hopper outside, my teacher returned to my desk and stood with her arm outstretched and her finger pointing toward the door. I knew what that meant. Everyone knew what that meant."

"Get out?" I asked.

"Not exactly," Grandma answered as more thunder rolled in. "It meant, 'Go to the Principal's office.'"

I sank back in my chair. I had never been sent to the principal's office, oh boy! That's a big consequence at my school. *Although,* I thought, *no one ever brought a frog to my school, so I wondered if that person would get sent there.*

Grandma interrupted my wondering.

"Off I went. It wasn't far, so I didn't have much time to get scared. I thought there would be only adults in the office, and that was the part that scared me, but no."

"No?" I asked. "Who was there?"

Grandma took a deep breath. "A hero. Six-year-old Ruby Bridges. A first grader, just like me."

"Why was she in the principal's office?" I asked.

"She was the reason for the big crowd outside." Grandma continued. "Ruby was black. My school had only white children before that year. When the law changed, and schools had to accept black and white children, some white people were angry, fearful, and loud."

I thought about that for a minute but could not figure it out.

"Grandma," I started, "that doesn't make any sense. Why were grown-ups afraid of a six-year-old?"

"People sometimes fear what they don't know, and these people did not know many African American people. In 1960 in New Orleans, this is how some adults acted," Grandma answered.

The wind blew harder, and the thunder grew louder. The rain started to splash on the porch overhang. We could hear the "splat, splat, splat" as it landed.

Thunder boomed so loudly that I jumped out of my chair and into Grandma's lap. She let me scoot up there. I always felt safer in Grandma's lap.

The rain came down in buckets. It seemed as if the skies suddenly opened, and an ocean poured out.

"Want to go inside?" Grandma asked.

I shook my head. "No," I answered. "I want to hear the end of the story."

"OK, my little love," Grandma answered, "here goes."

She took a deep breath and let it out.

"I stared at Ruby for a long time. After a minute, she looked up at me. We just stared and stared at each other. It seemed like forever. Like we had never seen another first grader in our lives before. And then, without saying a word, Ruby slid down the bench a little bit, giving me room to sit next to her. Which I did."

A flash of lightning. A crash of thunder. The storm was right overhead. I leaned in closer to Grandma. She didn't flinch.

"After I sat, she spoke to me. She told me her name was Ruby, and I told her my name was Betty. She told me the people outside were yelling about her, and she had to sit in the office until everything calmed down. She told me only one teacher in the school wanted to teach her."

A flash of lightning. Two seconds passed. The clap of thunder. The storm was moving away.

Grandma went on. "Ruby asked why I was in the office. I told her I had brought a frog to school. That made her giggle. But only for a minute."

A flash of lightning. Four seconds passed. The clap of thunder. The rain was slowing down.

"Those people outside are yelling about me," Grandma said, repeating what Ruby had told her that day, "they don't want me to go to school here."

"What else did Ruby tell you?" I asked.

"Ruby told me, very quietly, that she had only gone to school with children who had skin like hers. This was her first time in school with white people. And that the grown-ups outside were very, very angry about that. They had made signs that said she should return to her old school and stay with people who looked like her. She told me her father lost his job, and some grocery stores would not sell food to her mother because the people were so angry. Some parents removed their children from my school altogether. It took four policemen to help Ruby and her mother get through the crowd and into the school's front door."

I told Grandma that I did not understand. "If all these terrible things were happening, why didn't Ruby switch schools? Wasn't she scared?"

"She was scared," Grandma told me, "but, she was brave. The bravest girl I had ever met. The bravest person I have met to this day, in fact. She stood up to all those angry grown-ups yelling at her and her mother and walked right into that school anyway. You can't be brave or a hero without being scared first. Remember that."

I thought about Grandma's words. There was one more distant call of thunder and some light rain sprinkles. The clouds appeared thinner, and the sky started to lighten.

"I didn't know kids could be heroes," I said.

"Oh yes," Grandma replied, "not only did Ruby stand up for herself that day, but every day that year, she sat in a class alone with the only teacher that would accept her. She never gave up. Her teacher, Mrs. Henry, taught her alone in a classroom for that whole first-grade year. Slowly, more African American children enrolled at my elementary school, and people's attitudes started to change. Eventually, Ruby graduated from a desegregated high school, and her nieces and nephews followed in her footsteps."

The rain stopped altogether. The skies were lighter, and the sun was starting to peek out.

Grandma drank the last of her lemonade.

"I met a true hero that day, my little love," she said, "I am sure of it."

The sun was shining now, and the air felt thick and humid again. Crickets were chirping, and the heat from the yard was almost visible.

"May I have more lemonade, Grandma?" I asked.

Grandma smiled at me and picked up both of our cups.

"Absolutely."

THE LOST LUNCH BOX

SLAM!

Every day, the same walk, the same turns, the same spot at the long, gray cafeteria table, and then...*slam!* This is our daily lunchtime routine.

Bobby's class lines up at the doorway when the classroom bell rings at noon. They are restless. They are excited.

It is time for lunch.

Lunch is a welcome break from all the reading, writing practice, and number drills the children do all morning in room 3C at Morning Grove Elementary School.

Bobby raises his arm like a professional sports player, whirls me around like the second hand on a clock, and, faster and faster, completes at least five rotations before bringing me to an abrupt landing with a loud *THUD* on the tabletop. How many dents, scrapes, and scratches have I received from this? Three large dents (when Bobby landed me on a corner), five scrapes, and I can't count how many scratches. The once brightly colored race cars that decorated the door to my delicious insides are now faded and, in some places, peeling.

When Bobby found me, I was a sparkly yellow lunch box on a shelf with dozens like me. All the lunch boxes were lined up tall and hoped one day to go home with a child who would take care of us and bring us to school. We would keep their hot lunches hot and their cold lunches cold. We waited patiently and dreamed of being chosen.

Bobby and his dad wandered down my aisle slowly one late summer afternoon when the sun was still high, and it seemed like the evenings would never start. Those days were precious. Bobby and his friends enjoyed everything summer had to offer: swimming in the lake, hiking in the woods, and playing hide and seek until dinnertime.

They knew school was just around the corner, and if they were honest, the friends were excited to be together again in Room 3C at Morning Grove - but they did not want the summer to come to an end.

They all agreed that third grade was going to be exciting. Long division was the next topic in math, and it was challenging but fun; third graders used the larger playground at recess, and, most importantly, they were able to eat lunch in the cafeteria every day.

This, Bobby's dad announced on that sunny morning in their green-and-yellow kitchen, called for a brand-new lunchbox. So, they came to my store, and they walked down my aisle. Bobby and his dad continued to pick up lunch boxes and put them back down.

"This one is too blue."

"This one is too small."

Bobby picked up a black and gray checkerboard-meets-lightning-bolt design lunchbox. His Dad looked at the price tag and exclaimed, "this one is too expensive!"

Bobby didn't argue or complain; he simply put the lunchbox back on the shelf.

Choose me, I thought, *I will be the best lunch box you ever had!*

It must have been my bright yellow exterior that caught Bobby's eye. He walked directly to me and picked me up. He waved wildly to his father, still several paces back up the aisle, and called him over.

"This one!" Bobby was jumping up and down now. "The racecars! I want this yellow one!"

And that is how it started. Bobby was so excited to bring me home and show his mother what he and his father had bought. She lovingly cleaned me out with a warm, soapy cloth and set me on the rack to air dry. I wondered what the first lunch would be. A sandwich? Bagged crackers? Cookies? CANDY?

The first day of school arrived. I could hear Bobby in his bedroom with his mother choosing the all-important first-day-of-school outfit. It was clearly more important to his mother than to him. They decided together on blue jeans, a red t-shirt, and white tennis shoes to go with his black and gray backpack. I was happy; I would be the only yellow item.

After a warm breakfast, Bobby's mom took me down from the drying rack and started filling me up. What would it be?!

First…, a peanut butter and grape jelly sandwich. Standard, tried, and true. I heard Bobby say it was his favorite sandwich.

Next, an apple. As his mother put the apple inside, she smiled at Bobby, and Bobby frowned. "Cookies?" He asked with a frown, clearly unhappy with his mother's healthy choice.

Without looking away, Bobby's mother reached over the sink, grabbed a bag of chocolate chip cookies, and winked as she dropped them in. Bobby ran over and hugged her.

Oh! I remember that first day so clearly. I was so full of hope. So full of bright newness. Everything looked and smelled new. My plastic, the air in the school hallways, the freshly sharpened pencils in the classroom. The first few lunches were exciting.

Then the slamming started.

"DO IT, BOBBY!" the other boys yelled. "SEE IF IT BREAKS TODAY!"

Shortly after school began, Bobby stopped adoring my bright yellow exterior. The decal race cars. The cool white snap lock. Dad said Bobby had to use me for the whole school year - unless I broke - so each day at lunch, Bobby slammed me down before opening me. I was full of dents and scrapes by the second month of school.

Today was not the day. I braced myself as soon as Bobby came around the corner into the cafeteria and walked to his assigned seat. I could smell the hot lunch of the day. Hot dogs.

SLAM!

It was just once, just one *SLAM,* followed by a chorus of disappointed boys - "Boooooo!" Bobby slumped down in his seat. I know he wished my hinges had given out that day. Or that my handle had popped. Was he hoping his father would take him back to the store and buy him one of those other, snazzier lunch boxes to replace me?

Time passed. Pints of milk were opened, and some spilt. At some point, Bobby absentmindedly elbowed me to the side while he gobbled his food - dinner leftovers and a juice box. I was off to the side now. Across from no one.

The boy seated next to Bobby, Sam, brought baseball cards to lunch. As soon as he finished eating, he cleaned up and took them out of his pocket. Bobby, Sam, and their friend Roger loved the cards. Sam placed each lovingly on the cafeteria table while the boys pointed and chatted. Bobby's back was to me now while he asked this and that about the faces on the cards. They seemed very important to him.

Roger sneezed. Hard. Three times in a row. The cards went everywhere; under the table, onto empty seats, and on the floor. Roger, Sam, and Bobby rushed to clean them up just as the whistle blew to signal the end of lunch.

"LINE UP!" The teachers called, and the students jumped up to get the best spot in line.

The teachers marched the classes out of the cafeteria and back to the classrooms. But there I stayed. A forgotten yellow lunchbox. On the cafeteria table.

Mrs. Miller, one of the teachers who worked in the cafeteria, spotted me. I was hard to miss, after all, I was bright yellow.

"Well, look here," Mrs. Miller said, "someone forgot a lunchbox."

She picked me up, closed me carefully, and walked me over to the corner of the cafeteria.

This was it, I thought. *The end.*

The Lost and Found.

Mrs. Miller placed me on top. I was grateful she did not slam me, but I guess adults don't slam things as much as kids do, do they? She stepped back for a moment, looked at me, and then walked away. The cafeteria, so loud and bustling with movement moments before, was silent and still.

"Hey!" I heard a muffled voice from below. "Hey, you up there? Can you hear me?"

I could not believe what I was hearing. Was someone - or something? Talking to me?

"I can hear you," I said. "Who are you?"

"Pink Jacket, nice to meet you," she answered, "you are sitting on top of me, in case you hadn't noticed."

"I am Yellow Lunchbox. Bobby just left me here."

"You're in the Lost and Found," Pink Sweatshirt told me, "at the top, luckily. The ones on top are most likely to be picked up. The ones on the bottom...," her voice trailed off. I could barely hear the murmurs of others below her in the box.

"I've been here before," Pink Jacket continued. "I'm left behind a lot. But she always comes back for me. Stay hopeful!"

I had to admit, Pink Jacket sounded cheerful. But I was scared. And it was so quiet. I felt lonely without Bobby. Even with the slamming and wondering if I would be replaced, I never felt lonely.

The cafeteria lights went out. The lights were controlled by motion sensors and went off without movement in the cafeteria. I remembered Bobby's teacher telling the class about the new lights throughout the school. She told them it was better for the environment. Maybe. But now I was lonely, AND it was dark.

I tried to stay hopeful, as Pink Jacket told me. I thought about the day Bobby picked me up in the store and brought me home. I thought about all the lunches Bobby's mother and father had made and loaded and the excited look on Bobby's face when he opened me up to see what they had packed. I remembered the warm feeling of Bobby's hand when he carried me to and from school and the smell of cookies baking when Bobby walked me through the front door of my home.

Suddenly, the lights came on in the cafeteria. The memory of baking cookies vanished in the bright glare.

Pink Jacket perked up. "Oh my!" she said excitedly. "Someone came back!"

Was it Bobby?

I felt a hand around my handle. But it didn't pull me up. It pushed me aside. When the hand let go, I saw Pink Jacket float upward, giggling with glee. A girl's voice said, "Yup! This is the one!"

I was crushed.

"Now it's my turn!" A boy's voice called. It was Bobby.

Bobby had come back also.

"It's right on top!"

Bobby grabbed me with both hands and pulled me close.

He hugged me.

"I found you," he whispered.

We stood there for a moment, then turned to go back to class. And then later, we went home, where we were greeted at the door by the smell of freshly baked chocolate chip cookies.

SHE SHOOTS, AND SHE SCORES!

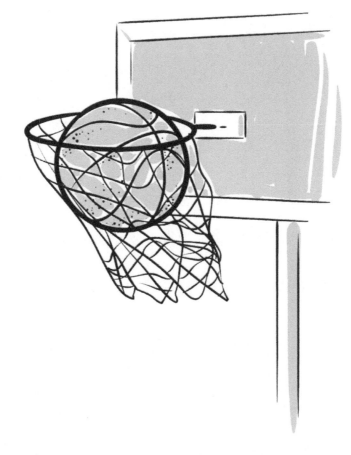

Layla laced up her sneakers and wondered how Maggie had convinced her to do this. *Is Maggie good at everything, even persuasion?* Layla thought.

Layla and Maggie were best friends. They did everything together, and they did it all: ice skating, crafts club, movies, and listening to music. Now they were playing school basketball together.

They signed their names on a yellow paper sheet outside Coach Cathy's office last Friday afternoon. Layla had tried to forget about it until the day of the first practice. Now Layla was in the locker room, telling herself it would all be over soon.

Maggie bounced by her.

"This is so exciting!" She said. "We are finally old enough to do after-school basketball!" She clapped and grinned from ear to ear. Other girls around them in the locker room looked up at the sound, then went back to getting ready.

"Will you please keep it down?" Layla begged. "This is embarrassing enough! I will look like I have two left feet out there!"

"NO way!" Maggie answered. "I will help you. It's just a friendly game between friends, and you'll see. It will be fun!"

They jogged out to the gym floor to see 20 other girls standing in a semi-circle around Coach Cathy. She was checking names off the list, and Maggie and Layla were the last to arrive.

"Good afternoon, ladies," Coach Cathy said with a smile, "and welcome to our first practice! Today is about getting to know your teammates and drills, drills, drills!"

She sounded so upbeat and excited, and for a moment, Layla was as well. She didn't know what drills were, but how bad could they be?

Drills meant exercises over and over, and Layla found herself passing the basketball back and forth to her teammate. Then the girls would rotate. Rotate. Pass. Rotate. Pass.

When Layla's arms were about to go numb, running drills started. First, there was a quick jog around the gym, followed by speed drills. Layla, Maggie, and the rest of the team ran as fast as they could to "mid-court" - a black line that cut the gym in half - then turned and raced back.

Layla was last every time.

Coach Cathy seemed delighted at the end of the first practice. She gave every girl a high five and said one contribution they could make to the team.

"You will be a real asset with your speed," she said to one girl named Gwen.

Gwen beamed.

"I can see you have a spot-on aim when passing!" She told Lamara.

Lamara replied, "Thank you, Coach!"

"Maggie, I saw the ball move quickly when you passed. That will outsmart the other team every time!"

"Thanks, Coach Cathy," Maggie smiled.

Coach Cathy stood next to Layla, the last player in the line.

"Layla," she said, smiling, and then stopped as if she forgot what she was going to say.

"Yes, Coach Cathy?" Layla responded.

"Layla," Coach Cathy put a hand on her shoulder, "I am happy to see you here today."

Then Coach Cathy walked to her office and closed the door.

The rest of the girls were chatting as they strolled toward the locker room. Maggie looked at Layla, who was confused.

"Happy I was here?" Layla said to her friend. "Couldn't she think of anything else to say?"

Maggie shrugged. She started to unbraid her hair and shake it out. "I think you were great out there!" Her friend beamed. "You really hustled during those running drills.

"I was last every time, Maggie."

Maggie countered: "So much room for improvement!"

At that, Layla giggled and said, "let's get some water. I am exhausted!"

At home, Layla helped her mother set the table for dinner. Her arms and legs were sore from the workout, and she couldn't wait to get into bed, but she also felt this slight sense of accomplishment: not everyone had completed a basketball workout that day. Layla felt proud.

"Tired?" Layla's Mom seemed to read her mind.

"You bet I am," Layla replied, placing another plate on the table. Her mother started handing her the flatware while her father finished cooking.

"You know," her mother started, looking over her should at Layla's father in the kitchen, "I used to play basketball in I was young, too."

"You did?" Layla asked.

"I sure did," her mother answered, "I wasn't any good. But I had fun playing."

Layla sighed. "I am not any good either."

Her mother walked over to her and took her chin in her hand.

"Layla, playing on a team is not about being *good*!" Her mother emphasized that last word. "It's about having fun, meeting people, getting some exercise, and did I say having fun?"

Layla's Mom kissed her cheek, and they finished setting the table together.

Layla and Maggie were practicing after school every day, and they met a new friend, Joy. They moved beyond drills into actual games, and Layla could confidently pass and dribble the ball. Within a few weeks, Layla could anticipate rebounds, which happen when someone shoots the ball at the net, and then it starts to land. Layla seemed to sense where the ball was going and could get there before anyone else; Coach Cathy began to call her "The Rebounder."

"Good game, Rebounder!" A girl named Michaela said to Layla after practice. Maggie jumped up and down, clapping. This time, Layla didn't stop her.

"This is so much fun!" Layla told her best friend.

"I told you it would be!" Maggie said. "I can't wait to practice shooting the ball a lot more."

Layla felt nervous at that thought. She'd improved at everything else - except shooting.

"I don't know," Layla started, "maybe I should stick to rebounding. I am good at that."

"Yeah, you are!" Maggie said, with tons of encouragement. Maggie was always the best cheerleader. "But maybe there is a great basketball shooter in there, and we must get her OUT!" Maggie shouted the last word, and both girls laughed at the echo.

Layla stood at the free throw line on Friday afternoon, and Maggie was with her. The other teammates had gone home, but Maggie had talked Layla into staying for extra shooting practice.

CLANK.

The ball bounced off the rim and back at Layla.

"Aim for the box on the backboard, not the net...," Coach Cathy told Layla for what seemed like the millionth time.

"That's what I am DOING!" Layla said, frustrated.

Maggie jogged over to the ball and picked it up. She raced back to the free throw line and demonstrated a perfect free throw for Layla.

"You make it look so easy," Layla said, "how do you doooooo that?" She was tired and achy, and Layla was sure she would not master this tonight. She took the basketball out of Maggie's hands, tried again, and got the same result. Layla could feel tears coming.

"OK, OK," Coach Cathy said, "enough for one day. There is something called over-practicing, and I think we are there."

Layla had a hard time falling asleep that night. She pictured Maggie over and over, making that free throw shot. How did she do it? It looked so simple - just bend at the knee, look at the box behind the net, spring, and shoot.

Layla's teammates were buzzing at practice the next day.

"What's going on?" Layla asked Maggie and Joy.

"We are going to play an actual, real game! Against a team in the next town!" Maggie was jumping up and down again.

"Who?" Layla asked.

"West School!" Joy answered.

"They've had a team for three years!" Layla answered. "We will get creamed!"

"Come on, Layla!" Maggie said. "Think about how much better you've gotten! A real basketball game could be so much fun! I am so excited!"

"You're always so excited!" said Joy.

The girls laughed.

The BIG GAME arrived. Layla's parents were in the gym, which was packed. Layla was nervous, but her nerves calmed when she realized she would not be one of the starting players. Maggie was on the court right away, as she was one of the best players on the team.

The whistle blew, and Layla clapped loudly for Maggie, Joy, and the other players. Despite the other team's experience, Layla's team kept pace with their scoring.

Layla came off the bench for a few minutes in the second quarter and made some great rebounds, and some even resulted in points for Layla's team. Layla could hear Coach

Cathy cheering for her as she ran back up the court. She was starting to feel like her team could win this game!

Layla was re-tying her sneakers in the fourth quarter when she heard the crowd let out a collective gasp. When she looked up, a group, including the school principal and Coach Cathy, surrounded a player.

That player...was Maggie!

Layla's heart started to pound quickly. She began to stand up when she felt Joy's hand on her arm.

"You can't go onto the court; it's not allowed!" Joy said, pulling on Layla's arm.

There were only ten seconds left in the game, but the clock was stopped by the injury delay.

Everything happened very quickly. The school principal and Coach Cathy helped Maggie off the court. Layla could see that Maggie was putting some weight on both feet, so nothing was broken, but she could also see the pain in her face.

Layla knew the game would have to resume in a few seconds because the injured player was off the court. Coach Carter was standing in front of her, and she was smiling.

"Layla," she said quietly, "Maggie is OK. Her ankle is badly sprained. She cannot play for the final seconds of the game. All we need" - the whistle blew again - "all we need, is for you to replace her. Our team gets two free throws now. If we make just one" - she held up one finger to make her point - "we win. You can do this and do it for Maggie."

Layla looked down the bench at Maggie. The school nurse was wrapping her ankle. Even in pain, she made eye contact with Layla, and mouthed, "you can do it!" And clapped her hands.

Coach Cathy held a hand out to Layla, encouraging her to stand and join her teammates. They were lined up on either side of the net. Most of the girls had their hands on their hips, waiting patiently for the game to continue.

Layla took the basketball and dribbled a few times, breathing slowly, trying to focus. She looked at the net, inhaled, and bent her knees. Then Layla loosened them and assumed the shooting position with her arms. Without taking her eyes off the box on the backboard, she took her shot - only to have it circle the net and fall off to the right, rolling away with small bounces. Layla closed her eyes.

The crowd responded with a short "oh!!" followed by applause and a few shouts of "You can do it, Layla!"

Layla felt fully refreshed, centered, and confident when she opened her eyes. She bent her knees, brought her arms up, and locked her eyes on the backboard.

She took her shot.

The basketball circled the rim and seemed to stop in place for an entire second. The crowd held its breath.

And then, the basketball dropped through the net! After a second of silence, the crowd started to cheer.

Joy was the first one off the bench, and she hugged Layla so tightly Layla thought she might pop. Coach Cathy ran onto the floor as the game-ending whistle blew, and Layla's team came out on top. Cathy hugged Layla and told her she was proud of her. Maggie limped onto the floor and hugged her friend.

Maggie whispered to Layla, "I told you it would be fun!"

WHEN I WAS YOUNG, A POEM

When I was young, life was so sweet
I had a friend on every street
We ran and played and sang and slept
And joked and laughed until we wept

Long before, in baby years
There were so many, many tears
Anything could make me cry
A noise, the dark, a dove's sweet sigh

But also, small things made me laugh
My mama's smile, my stuffed giraffe
The sound of rain upon the roof
My older brother acting a goof

As I grew older, I outgrew clothes
And starting growing like a rose
My papa said he could not believe
How tall I'd become one New Year's Eve

I started school on a crisp fall day
With pens and paper, I was on my way
A brand-new dress with shoes to match
And chocolate cookies from a freshly baked batch

New friends, new work, new things to learn
Surprises around every turn

In a brand-new place to stay all-day
And a brand-new place in which to play

Learn I did, spelling and math
History and science on a whole new path
Snack time, lunchtime, quiet time, too
So many things to see and do

In the night, when the sun was low
When there was nowhere left to go
I'd stay at home and feel carefree
To sit and think and smile and be

Then time for bed and I would sleep
Fast and still and oh so deep
I'd dream of having not one care
Peacefully quiet in the nighttime air

Change then came into my life
As I grew older and learned of strife
Homework and squabbles and chores each day
Although I tried to wish them away

School became harder
For days I would ponder
On writing and Latin and numbers, oh
Wishing for an easier go

Friends and weekends were still fun
Still playing, smiling, on the run
Movies, games, sleepovers too
Always something fun to do

When I was ten we moved away
To a new town where I would stay
New friends, new school, new places to go
New routines to undergo

With time I grew to love my new home
And no longer felt the need to roam
Here I could stay and here I could grow
Until there was another place to go

But childhood lasts only so long
Some days as fleeting as a song
As I neared the age of ten
I thought of growing young again

Of sunny days and happy times
And sitting in laps and reading rhymes
Learning to crawl, learning to count
It made me glad, a good amount

Friendship, kinship, playtime fun
Together when the day is done

Thinking of those special places
Spent in childhood, my heart still races.

THE END

SMALL, BUT SAVES ALL

Gabby first saw the bright light traveling through the sky while walking home from school on a sunny Tuesday afternoon. She held her backpack, lunchbox, and jacket. The morning had been chilly, and the sky was full of clouds; now, the sun shone brightly, and the clouds were gone.

Gabby's lunchbox featured her favorite superhero, Gold Girl, who was tough as nails, more potent than any human, and could fly with speed and grace. She wore a gold leotard and a headband with a large "GG" on it. Gabby liked to think it might stand for "Gabby Girl."

The light was a bright yellow color, and for a moment, Gabby could picture 'Gold Girl' jetting through the sky. Was she on her way to save someone?

And then Gabby wondered, *What IS that yellow light?* She stopped on the sidewalk, mere houses from her own, and watched the light as it glided across the sky and, in an instant, stopped and silently exploded in a flash so bright that it knocked Gabby over. When she sat up on the sidewalk, the light was gone.

Gabby looked around quickly, but no one else saw what had happened. She quickly gathered up her things and kept walking toward home.

The side door was unlocked when she arrived home.

"Mi Vida!" Her mama, Ana, exclaimed when Gabby opened the door. "How was school today?"

"Alright," Gabby answered, still a bit dizzy from what she had just experienced.

Her mother noticed. "Are you alright, my dear?" Ana asked, holding Gabby's chin in her hand and looking closely at Gabby's eyes.

"Yes, yes, I feel fine," Gabby replied, pulling her face away, "I saw something weird while I walked home from school."

Her mother frowned. "Weird?" She asked. "Like, weird, how?"

Gabby shrugged. "There was a light in the sky. Moving in the sky. Crossing the sky."

Ana looked concerned. She wiped her hands on a kitchen towel and sat by the table. Delicious smells wafted out of the oven, and the sink was full of soapy dishes.

"Was it anything like a plane or a big bird?" Ana asked.

"No, nothing like that," Gabby shook her head. "It was like...," she tried to picture it again, but she couldn't even see it in her mind's eye.

"Gabby," Ana began, "are you sure, and I mean sure, you didn't hit your head yesterday?"

Ana had asked Gabby that question at least a hundred times in the past 24 hours. Yesterday there had been an earthquake. It was a small, wall-shaking, no-big-deal earthquake. Gabby had not even fallen to the ground, much less hit her head. She and her friends had been outside when it happened.

They were in the field behind the playground during recess time, enjoying the sun, and running around. There was a sound like a low tremble of thunder. Kids started to look at each other with puzzled looks on their faces. Realization spread quickly. It was not the first time an earthquake had hit the town of San Capique.

Outside? The earthquake safety poster in the hallway read, *STAY OUTSIDE!*

Gabby remembered it clearly as she shouted to her friends, "Run over here!" She jumped up and down and waved her arms in the air. Children ran off the playground and into the field while the ground started to tremble. Gabby knew to stay in an open outdoor space when an earthquake started. Gabby looked around. The field was the flattest, most open space.

Teachers helped the younger children move quickly away from the buildings, across the playground, and into the field, and then - it was over almost as soon as it began. There were no injuries. Even so, nervous parents like Gabby's came to the school that afternoon to bring her home.

"But now you are seeing things?" Ana asked her daughter.

"I am not 'seeing things,'" Gabby answered her mother, "just a light in the sky. It was nothing. I have homework to do. I will see you at dinner."

Gabby marched up the steps with her backpack to her bedroom and shut the door. She thought she lightly pushed it closed but was startled when it slammed so loudly her mother came bounding up the stairs and demanded she opened it up.

"No slamming doors in this house! You know the rule!" Ana was angry.

"I didn't!" Gabby protested. "I mean, I didn't think I did. I didn't mean to. I am sorry."

Ana turned and walked back to the kitchen, and Gabby could hear Ana washing dishes and continuing with dinner.

That was weird, Gabby thought, dropping her backpack and slouching into her desk chair. She decided she wanted to rest before starting her homework, so she slid over to her bed and got comfortable, and dozed off.

About an hour later, she could hear her mother's voice calling her.

"Gabby? Honey? Please set the table for dinner! Can you hear me? Gabby?"

Gabby opened one eye slowly and then another. She had a strange, unsettled feeling in her stomach. She felt like…like…

There was nothing below her. She was hovering *over* her bed.

She looked down and could clearly see her bed: the pillow, her teddy bear, the blanket, and the little doll her grandmother had made for her, for her last birthday. She knew if she reached down, she could touch them. But there she hovered, wondering what was happening.

"Gabby?" Ana called again. "Gabs? Did you hear me?"

"Yes, Mama!" Gabby said, sitting on the air above her bed. "I will be down in a minute!"

Upon saying the word "down," her body gently lowered itself to the bed. *OK*, Gabby thought, *I am down. I wonder what happens if ….?*

And as she thought the word "up," up her body went! She was hovering over her bed again. When she looked at her hands, that same yellow light, like the one she had seen streaking across the sky earlier that day, was shining all around her fingers and arms, tracing them.

OK, OK, Gabby thought. *I can go up and down, but what if ….?*

Slowly she floated up to her ceiling, stopped, and thought about moving around her room. Her body followed her brain's commands.

Whoa, Gabby thought. *I CAN FLY!*

"Gabby!" Ana yelled. "Set the table this minute!"

"Coming, Mom!" Gabby replied, and she opened her bedroom door and ran down the stairs.

In what seemed like no time at all, she grabbed a few things from the kitchen cabinets, ran around the table, and stopped. Her mother turned from taking dinner out of the oven. She almost dropped dinner.

"Gabby!" she exclaimed. "How did you do that so quickly?"

"I—I—don't know," Gabby stammered, I just…just…did."

That night in her bed, after her parents had gone to sleep. Gabby thought about the last few days.

1. *There was an earthquake at school*
2. *I saw a crazy light in the sky, which grew so large and bright it knocked me down*
3. *Later that afternoon, I realized I was extra strong (kicking the door closed)*
4. *I realized I can fly*
5. *I had super speed*

Could these things be related? Gabby thought as she drifted off to sleep.

The next morning, Gabby woke up to the sound of the news on the television downstairs. Her parents always watched the news before work.

"While the earthquake was small and did little damage, and there was no repeat yesterday, residents are still being cautioned today, as bigger earthquakes may follow…."

Gabby's father snapped the television off. "Have some breakfast, Gabby," he told her, "and then, off to school."

"And be careful. You heard what the TV said about earthquakes! You were lucky the other day!" Ana said.

Lucky? Gabby thought. *I sure was…, something.*

Gabby walked to school at her usual pace, exchanging happy hellos with friends and teachers when she arrived at school. Morning work passed normally. It was time for recess.

One of Gabby's teachers led her third-grade class outside. The sun was as bright. Just like the day of the earthquake.

Gabby and a few of her friends spread out in the field with a large purple ball and started playing bounce-catch. As Erika turned toward Joe, the first rumble started. Students froze. Gabby was perfectly peaceful. She looked immediately at her hands. They were glowing yellow. What exactly what happening? She wasn't sure, but the ground was starting to shake.

Her classmates looked at each other nervously.

"Stay calm, everyone," Gabby said, "we are in the safest place we can be. Let's call the kids on the playground over!" She turned to shout, "Come over here! Quick!" The little ones were too frightened to move, and the ground was shaking harder.

Before Gabby knew it, she had run across the field in no time at all. And her sneakers were glowing yellow! She grabbed four or five kids and thought *UP*. Much to everyone's surprise - including Gabby's - she flew back to the middle of the field and gently placed the surprised children on the trembling ground. Older students ran over to hold the scared children's hands as Gabby flew off again.

It was like a dream. Gabby made the trip five times. She picked up several teachers on the last trip, as the trembles turned to rumbles and great shakes. Suddenly, a sound like cars crashing and steel bending reached Gabby's ears. She turned to face her school.

The ground next to the third-grade rooms had started to cave in, and the wall had begun to buckle. The doors from the classrooms to the outdoors bent, and Gabby knew her friends in those rooms would be trapped.

I can fly. I am strong. I am fast. Gabby realized all of these things must have come from the bright light she had seen while walking home from school the day before. She still didn't know how everything was connected, but that didn't matter right now; people were in trouble and Gabby could help.

"UP!" Gabby said aloud and thought about getting to the classrooms in trouble. Her friends in the field, still comforting the scared younger students, watched in awe as she hovered above the damaged wall. Gabby quickly determined how bad the damage was, and waited for the next rumble to pass.

She could see into the first classroom. It was another third grade. Several of the students there were her friends, and she could see how scared they were. The teacher had instructed them to go under their desks like it was a drill, but this was real. Some students were crying. Some were talking to themselves. When they saw Gabby hovering in the space where the wall had separated from the ceiling, they became very quiet and wide-eyed.

Gabby's entire body glowed yellow, and her hands were on her hips. The land settled, and she wondered if it was over, or only between tremors. She decided to take advantage of the lull. She grabbed the bricks closest to her and pulled. They easily pulled away from the wall. Gabby knew she had to make a stable, safe opening to get the students out.

She double-checked that no one was behind and below her on the ground, and in no time at all, Gabby had pulled hundreds of bricks away. Then she started making trips into the classroom, picking up students, and flying them to the middle of the field. Back and forth, back and forth. On the last trip, she took the teacher and her aide. Then, she flew back and repeated what she had done for the other third-grade classroom. Within minutes, the entire third grade and teachers were safe in the middle of the field.

Gabby was still glowing yellow. She flew around the building to see if there was any other damage. Luckily, only that wall had buckled, and the tremors were quieting and growing farther apart. She made one last circle around the school, scouting for injured people but found none. There was one last rumble of the earthquake as she flew. Gabby heard a tremendous crash and saw a plume of smoke rise through the air.

Gabby reversed course. When she rounded the corner, she saw that the buckled wall had caved in. Gabby had saved the two classes with her newfound powers. She looked at her glowing hands, and the ground far beneath her, with surprise.

Everything became quiet. For a moment, Gabby could hear birds chirping in the trees again, then she heard the sounds of children clapping and cheering for her.

The students ran across the field to Gabby, as she slowly floated to the ground. The children hugged her and the adults thanked her and asked how she did it. Gabby couldn't answer them. The yellow glow had disappeared. She felt firmly connected to the ground again.

Gabby instinctively looked up. A small, fast, yellow light was gliding across the sky, and for a moment, all sound faded away. Gabby watched it until it was out of sight. It didn't explode into a bright light this time.

Did that mean Gabby would keep her powers?

CASE CLOSED

Alan threw the stick again for DC to fetch. It was a warm sunny day in Wyndsville, perfect for an outdoor game. DC, a lean and tough German Shepard puppy with a perfect sense of smell, ran after the stick. Alan loved his dog unconditionally; DC and Alan had been best friends for a year. Alan had taught DC to sit, shake hands, and fetch on command.

DC ran to Alan with the stick in his mouth, smiling his goofy dog smile. *A perfect day*, Alan thought to himself.

Just then, Harley ran into Alan's yard.

"Alan!" Harley called, excited and out of breath. "You won't believe what I just heard in the library!"

"Hey, Harley," Alan said. Harley was always excited about something, and Alan knew never to get worked up until he knew the specifics when she was involved.

Harley put her hands on her knees and paused to catch her breath. "There was," she breathed, "art," she stopped to breathe again, "stolen."

"Stolen?" Alan repeated, "what do you mean, stolen?"

"What do you think I mean?" Harley practically shouted, hands on her hips. "Stolen! You know, when someone takes something that doesn't belong to them? STOLEN!"

"Who would steal art from the Wyndsville Art Museum?" Alan remained calm, despite Harley's near hysterics.

"I don't know." Harley's hands were up in the air now. "That's what we have to find out!"

"Slow your roll," Alan said, "why do WE have to find out?"

"Because we're the 'Crime Solvers,' remember?" Harley gave a big grin.

Alan remembered. He remembered a few weeks ago when a little kid had shoplifted a bag of candy from the general store in town, and he and Harley had figured out who did it and walked the kid back to the store before he had a chance to eat it.

"Big deal," Alan said. "We solved that with luck."

"And your super sniffing dog here," Harley jerked a thumb at DC.

DC let out a bark then, seemingly to agree with Harley. He was eager to get on another case!

"OK, OK," Alan said. "Slow down and tell me what you know. Then I will decide if we even have another case to solve!"

Harley took two deep breaths and straightened her back. She wanted to present the facts in the best possible light and solve another case with Alan. She'd had fun working with Alan and DC, and Harley just knew they were the team for this stolen art job!

"I was looking for the next two mystery books from the *It's All Elementary* series, the one I was telling you about," Harley started. That series taught kids how to notice clues and solve mysteries, and Harley was hooked. "The library was super quiet, so I could clearly hear two research librarians talking in the stacks behind me. Verna, the tall one with the glasses who tells us to be quiet or get out all the time …."

Here Alan cut in, "OH HER? She is so mean!"

"Yes, HER," Harley answered, "anyway, Verna told Sally, the shorter librarian who lets us eat in the children's sections, that a painting was stolen last night, and it was there at 10 p.m. when the museum closed, and it was missing when the museum opened this morning at 10 a.m."

"Huh," Alan said, somewhat intrigued. He wasn't hooked yet. "Go on. Any clues?"

"Of course!" Harley said, hands on hips again. "There are always clues."

Alan nodded. Of course, there were.

"One: There were crumbs on the floor from the wall where the painting was to right out the back door."

"What kind of crumbs?" Alan asked, a little more interested.

"I don't know!" Harley practically shouted. "How would I know that, Alan?"

DC nudged Alan's hand again, so Alan picked up a stick and threw it for him. Off DC went to fetch.

"Anything else?" Alan asked.

"Two," Harley continued, "there was a dent in the floor, which is halfway between the bare spot on the wall and the back door."

"That's interesting," Alan admitted. That was a good clue.

"AND…," Harley started as DC came trotting back. She gave him a scratch behind the ears, and he licked her hand. "The alarm never went off. So, I already assume it was an inside job."

Alan thought about that for a minute.

"Maybe," he said finally, "maybe not. Let's not assume anything until we see where these clues lead us. Let's head to the museum."

Harley's eyes widened. "Does that mean you are IN?" She asked excitedly.

"I am in," Alan said, shaking her hand and throwing the stick again for DC to fetch.

Alan and Harley walked with DC on his leash down Main Street to the Wyndsville Art Museum.

The last time they were there had been a class trip, and Alan remembered it was musty and dull. He was not looking forward to going inside again, but he knew how much this meant to Harley.

Harley, on the other hand, could barely contain her excitement. She couldn't wait to examine the spot where the picture had been, especially the dent on the floor.

The two kids and the puppy climbed the steps and opened the thick, wooden door to the museum. Yes, the musty smell was still there. There were not a lot of patrons in the building, and a few police officers were asking questions of people who worked there.

"No dogs allowed!" Shouted Kent Lemons, one of the curators. He usually sat by the front desk to greet guests but had a sour disposition and a frown. He saw DC coming inside and immediately wanted to stop him.

"I can't leave him alone outside, Mr. Lemons," Alan told him, "he's well-behaved and won't bark or bother anyone."

"It's true, Mr. Lemons," Harley chimed in innocently, "this dog appreciates good art!"

Alan snickered.

Kent relented and said, "Fine, fine, fine. Just keep the puppy quiet, or else you all have to leave!" He sat behind his desk and returned to his magazine, *Weightlifting Weekly*.

DC started pulling on his leash. He didn't usually pull unless he smelled something he wanted to find, so Alan allowed him a little slack on his leash. Whatever smelled good was in Mr. Lemons' garbage can.

As casually as possible, the kids walked over to the garbage pail and peeked in. There were many crumpled-up papers, an old pen, and an empty carton of chocolate chip cookies.

"DC must've smelled the cookies," Alan whispered to Harley, "I thought no one was allowed to eat in the museum."

Harley just shrugged. Alan tugged a little on DC's leash, and they kept walking.

Alan and Harley pretended to wander around the museum, then stopped at the bare spot on the wall where the stolen painting had been.

Only two officers were left at the museum, and Harley and Alan hoped to overhear their conversation. The employee interviews were over, but some people still spoke to the police. Alan noted several mysterious adults.

"Well, Bob, I can't figure it out," said the first officer.

"Me either, Rob," said the second.

"Crumbs, a heavy painting is gone, and no alarm," Bob said. "All seems odd."

Alan leaned close to Harley, who pretended to look at a fruit painting. They didn't find out anything after talking to everyone who worked here.

Harley kept looking at the painting. "They said the picture was heavy, so either a strong person stole it, or more than one person stole it."

Alan thought about that. "Right. It had to be heavy if it made a dent in the floor."

"Which also means," Harley looked straight at Alan, "the thief dropped the painting on the way out!"

Alan wasn't sure how that could be helpful, but it was something.

Mr. Lemons walked into the room then, or rather, hobbled. His right foot was bandaged, and he used a cane. He still had his *Weightlifting Weekly* magazine under his arm. He talked quickly with the police officers.

They were quiet, and although Harley and Alan tried to listen, they couldn't hear anything.

Except for a name - "Mr. Clark."

The police left as Alan and Harley moved to the next painting with DC. It was a family portrait, and it looked like it was from the 1800s.

Once the room was empty, DC hurried over to where the stolen painting had been. He sniffed the floor and then started licking it.

"No! Stop!" Alan said. Dogs shouldn't eat things off the floor; it could make them sick.

Harley rushed over to see what it was.

"Crumbs," she said, "just crumbs, Alan," she picked a few up, examined them in her hand, and then sniffed them.

"Wow, Alan, DC is good!! These are chocolate chip cookie crumbs!"

"CRUMBS!" Mr. Lemons shouted, and no one heard him sneak up on them. "Are you eating in my museum?"

"No, sir!" Alan insisted. But it was too late. Mr. Lemons was angry and wanted the kids and their dog to leave.

"Out! All of you out!" He pointed toward the door.

For a second, Harley saw a brightly colored wristband that said *Wyndsville Gym* on it. Did Mr. Lemons exercise?

On their way out, they passed a gentleman dressed in a spiffy navy suit. He wore a hat and looked very important.

"Ah, Mr. Clark," they heard Mr. Lemons say as they reached the exit, "how nice of you to come to the museum. What did you say that piece of art was worth?"

The sun was sliding low in the sky. Alan was expected home soon. DC needed his dinner, and Harley had a long walk back to her house. They discussed what they had discovered at the museum.

"You know what's weird," Harley started, "I never thought of old Mr. Lemons as someone who worked out! He seems so, so, not the type!"

They both laughed. DC barked in agreement.

"I know!" Alan said. "And reading *Weightlifting Weekly*? That guy? So stuffy!"

They were silent for a minute. Alan could tell Harley was deep in thought.

"Why do you think Mr. Lemons had a bandage on his foot?" Harley asked Alan.

Alan thought. "He was reading a weightlifting magazine, and we just figured out that he works out at the Wyndsville Gym, so maybe he dropped a weight on it."

There was more silence while they thought.

Harley sat in the grass and started pulling at it. "I can't put all the pieces together. That Mr. Clark was mysterious." Harley looked back at the museum. Mr. Clark and Mr. Lemons were locking up the entrance together. "I feel like all the pieces are right in front of us."

Me, too," Alan agreed. "The solution is right there on the tip of my tongue."

"Maybe we should go home, have a good night's sleep, and meet on this spot tomorrow.

"Great idea."

The next day, Alan and Harley met with DC on his leash on the grassy spot outside the museum. Mr. Lemons was about to open up for the day, and a few visitors were waiting on the steps.

"Hi, Harley," Alan said as DC barked.

"Hi, Alan, hi, DC," Harley answered, "wait here; I have an idea."

Harley jogged to the museum entrance as Mr. Lemons reached the top step. He turned his key in the door, and Harley followed him inside. A few seconds later, she came back out with a massive grin on her face. DC jumped up, feeling her excitement.

"Alan, I've got it!" She said. "Mr. Lemons knows the alarm code! That's the last clue we need!"

Alan stared at her with a puzzled look on his face. He had a feeling Mr. Lemons was the thief, but how?

Harley had her hands on her knees again, out of breath from running. "OK, I'll start," she said. "The crumbs on the floor near the bare spot on the wall were chocolate chip cookies, and the smell coming from the garbage next to Mr. Lemons' desk was …."

"From an empty container of chocolate chip cookies! Good work, DC!!" Alan kissed his puppy between his ears.

"By itself, that doesn't prove anything," Harley said, "except that Mr. Lemons probably broke his own 'No eating in the museum' rule. But that got me thinking. The police said there were crumbs leading from the spot on the wall OUT of the museum, and that's incriminating."

"Yes, it is!" Alan cried, a finger in the air.

"And if the painting was heavy enough to make a dent in the floor...."

"....when he dropped it!" Alan interrupted.

"That's right!" Harley continued. "He probably dropped it on his foot first, resulting in the bandage and the cane!

"But working out and reading the weightlifting magazine," Alan said, "he probably thought he could do it alone!"

"The part I can't figure out though...," Harley's voice trailed off for a second, "why would he steal from his own museum?"

Alan was silent. No, that didn't make sense to him either.

Then he figured it out.

"He's an art dealer! Mr. Lemons asked Mr. Clark how much the painting was worth. I bet he is an art dealer, and Mr. Lemons was going to SELL the painting!"

The two ran to the police station with DC. When they arrived, Detective Wayne took all their information and typed it into their computer, then thanked them for coming in.

"You and your dog DC cracked the case!" Detective Wayne told them. "You saved the day!"

101

Alan and Harley high-fived each other.

Detective Wayne stood up. "Now, if you will excuse me, you've given me enough information to arrest the suspect! We have cracked the case. In fact, I think the case is closed."

"Did you hear that, Harley?" Alan exclaimed. "CASE CLOSED!"

FROM DINOSAURS TO DOORS

"Catch me!" David yelled as he ran through Charles's backyard sprinkler. It was a steaming hot day, and both boys were in swim trunks and water shoes, playing in the backyard. David's puppy Whitey was outside with them. Whitey loved running through the water also, but he could not keep up with these rambunctious boys. He let out a few barks and stopped watching them run in circles when he grew tired.

Mom interrupted them, "lunch in half an hour!" She called out. "Ham and cheese sandwiches, OK?"

Both boys flashed David's mom the thumbs-up sign without stopping once. She disappeared into the house to start.

Suddenly, Charles was flat on his back on the grass. David was suspicious. Was this a new trick to make him get close, only to have Charles spring up and tackle him? It had happened before.

"OW!" David heard Charles yell, and David knew Charles was not joking around. He ran over to his friend, who was sitting up, rubbing his ankle.

"What happened?" David asked. "Are you OK?" His face was tight with concern.

Charles kept rubbing his ankle. "I tripped," he was close to tears, "but I'll be ok."

"Should I get my mom?" David asked with increasing concern.

"No, I said I would be ok," Charles said, now trying to move his ankle in small circles.

David wasn't sure Charles was fine, so he tried changing the subject. "What made you fall down, anyway?" He asked his friend.

Charles looked around. He was not one to trip over his own two feet. He was strong for a nine-year-old and played soccer and baseball at school, and people considered him the best athlete in the grade.

Something caught David's eye - it was a box. Charles had tripped over a wooden box in his yard, but what was a box doing in the grass?

David reached for the box, and Charles watched closely, still rubbing his ankle. For a moment, they just stared at it together.

"What is that? Why is it here?" Charles asked. "Has it been here the whole time?"

David did not know the answers to any of those questions. "No idea, he said, "but let's open it."

The box was unlocked, and there was a key inside. The key was shiny brass, with green stones embedded at the top. David turned the key around and around, looking for a word or tag. What did this key unlock?

"What does it unlock?" Charles asked, reading David's mind. David shrugged.

Behind them, a green glow came from the woods next to David's house. David's mom and dad had told him not to go into the woods because they feared he would lose his way. But something said to both boys the green glow and the green stones were connected, and they wanted to find out what was happening.

Charles stood up and gingerly put some weight on his twisted ankle. It was sore, but he could walk.

"Can you make it to the woods?" David asked Charles.

"I think, I can," Charles answered.

They walked away from the house and toward the trees. The green glow seemed to grow brighter. The trees started blocking the sun, and the air became chillier.

Within steps, David and Charles saw a green door glowing brightly. It was warm, too. There was a shiny brass keyhole, and David leaned forward with the key. It turned quickly in the lock, and the green door swung open.

Charles and David saw a vast lake in front of them. It was almost as large as an ocean, but far off in the distance, they could see that land wrapped all the way around. It was still and quiet for a moment until, from their right, a tremendous but slow thumping began. Slowly the boys looked toward the direction of the sound.

Dinosaurs! Plant-eating, long-necked, slow-moving dinosaurs were walking in front of them toward the edge of the water.

"Brachiosaurs," Charles uttered under his breath.

Neither boy could move; they simply stood watching the majestic creatures walk to the water and start drinking. There were dozens. David looked behind him, but the door was gone, and there were only trees. Panic flooded his body.

"Charles," he whispered, "Charles! The door is gone!"

Charles finally peeled his eyes away from the dinosaurs and looked over his shoulder. His jaw dropped, and his eyes became big as saucers.

"How are we going to get out of here?" Davis asked, and Charles shrugged.

"Do you still have the key?" Charles asked.

"How will a key help us if there is no door?" David yelled. The dinosaurs didn't notice David raising his voice.

Above them, pterodactyls flew and screeched, and the missing door was forgotten for a moment.

But only a moment.

A great roar came from the same direction as the brachiosaurs, and it was a vicious, angry, hungry-sounding roar. The sound was so strong that the trees started to bend.

107

David and Charles fell silent, and their hearts started beating hard.

Whatever was making that noise, neither boy wanted to hang around and see what it was.

They ran back into the woods, away from the noise, and the trees again blocked out the light. As Charles was wondering where they were going, David said, "Look! Another green glow!"

He pointed to the right, and the boys started running in the glow's direction. David was clutching the key and could still hear the faint sound of the roaring animal when they reached the glowing green door. David put the key into the lock, and the door swung open.

Immediately, the boys were blinded by a bright sun. David tried shielding his eyes, and Charles looked down. He realized he had no pain in his ankle. *Interesting*.

After his eyes adjusted to the light, David noticed how dry the air was. By the lake, the air was humid and almost tropical; it was nearly sharp here. His throat reacted merely seconds later, and thirst overtook him. He squinted and looked around. Charles put David's thoughts into words:

"I am so thirsty!"

What did David see? The air seemed to bend in the dry heat. It was difficult to see clearly, as heat wafted off..., was that sand everywhere?

"Of course, you're thirsty," David said, looking over his shoulder for the door that wasn't there, "we're in the desert."

"What's that funny-shaped building?" Charles said, pointing straight ahead.

"Those are actually a group of buildings, and they're called pyramids," David answered, "we learnt about them in school last year, remember?"

"So, we're in Egypt now?" Charles asked, not believing what he saw. "At least we moved up in years, and there are humans around now. I don't see any right here, exactly, but…." His voice trailed off as he shaded his eyes with his right hand and looked around. "Huh," Charles continued, "no people around. Anywhere. And we are in the middle of the desert. I have a bad feeling about this."

"Does your ankle hurt again?" David asked.

"No," Charles answered. "My ankle is fine. Good as new, actually." He hopped on one foot to show David how good it felt. "But out here in the heat, all alone, this is not a good situation."

"You think?" David said, looking around for anything that would be helpful. *Water? Nope. A door? Nope. Grown-ups to help us? Nope on that one, too.*

Then, in the distance, Charles saw a line of camels walking on behind the next. Tall men sat on top of each, holding a rein in his hand, steering the camel toward the Great Pyramids.

"Charles, do you know what is inside those pyramids?" David asked.

"I don't think I want to," Charles answered, and he felt a chill run down his spine, despite the heat.

Neither David nor Charles wanted to be seen by the men on the camels, but there was nowhere to hide. David looked down at the key in this hand and wished he could see a glowing door with a brass lock. He closed his eyes and pictured one in the sand, standing there, waiting to be opened.

It was too late. The men on the camels spotted David and Charles and changed direction to move toward them. They were shouting angrily. The boys looked at each other and then around. Way off behind them, near a tall dune, they spotted a glowing green door.

They ran off, kicking sand behind them, panting all the way.

The camels were faster than either boy imagined, and they gained on the boys quickly.

"Come on, come on!" Charles yelled to David. "We have got to get to that door!"

David tripped, fell onto the sand, and felt its scorching heat under his palms. He could hear the voices getting closer by the second.

Charles helped David up, and together they started for the glowing green door.

They made it!

Then, David dropped the key into the sand.

It sank like a stone and disappeared.

David and Charles looked at each other for a split second, then dropped to their knees and started digging furiously. The sand burned their fingertips, but they didn't slow down. The men on camelback weren't slowing either.

"I HAVE IT!" Charles declared and raised the key out of the sand triumphantly. He lunged for the lock. Charles turned the key quickly, and the door swung open. The boys jumped through. They heard the door slam shut, and everything went silent.

Black and silent.

David had a funny feeling in his stomach, and he wasn't quite dizzy but not entirely settled, either. The sensation reminded him of his first roller coaster ride. He heard Charles say something, but his voice sounded like he was underwater.

"David, look!" Charles managed. David looked over his left shoulder and saw...Earth. But how could that be? He looked at his feet, barely touching the grey rocks underneath. He and Charles were floating on the moon in less gravity than Earth, and it was a unique and not uncomfortable sensation. Seeing their world in the distance, however, was shocking. Neither of them could speak.

It was beautiful, really. For a minute neither boy felt fear or dread, but both were overwhelmed with awe. They looked once more at each other, and once more at the shining green and blue planet in the distance. They wondered silently how they arrived on the moon and how they would get home.

To the left, a green glow arose. Both boys slowly peered. It was a door, of course. A green, glowing door. Charles was still holding the brass key in his right hand, along with a few grains of sand from the desert.

The boys half-floated, half-swam through the air toward the door. When they arrived, they both took another minute to stare at the Earth. Then, Charles turned the key in the brass lock of the door. It slowly, very slowly, opened.

The boys peered through. They saw David's backyard. They saw the sprinkler, his puppy, and even his mother setting out the plate of cheese sandwiches and cups of juice she had promised earlier. They floated through the door and when their feet touched the ground again, they were back in their swimsuits and water shoes. They were standing at the edge of the woods.

David's mom looked up.

"Boys, have you been playing in the woods?" She asked, hands on hips, "you know how I feel about that! You could get lost! Or worse!"

David and Charles stepped forward, a little shaky from the return of gravity under their feet. They shuffled closer to the deck and mumbled apologies.

"Where were you for half an hour?" Mom asked, passing napkins around the table. "I looked out here and you were gone."

"We took a quick walk," Charles answered, "a pre-lunch stroll. I twisted my ankle and I wanted to stretch it out."

Mom looked at them both suspiciously.

"OK, then. No harm done, I guess," she responded, "you both seem fine to me," she winked at David, "how is your ankle, Charles?" Mom asked.

Charles answered, "It is…fine, actually," he sounded surprised himself, "it's really fine."

"I wonder how it got better so quickly," Mom said, "must've been quite a walk you just took."

"Yes, Mom," David said, looking at Charles, "we sure did have quite a walk!"

113

ROAD TRIP!

Pepper ran in circles, and baby Ali pretended to help dad load suitcases on top of the camper. *She wasn't* really *a baby*, Alex thought. Alex was nine, and Ali was three, so she clearly remembered when Ali was actually a little baby. There were diapers, bottles, and lots of crying. Alex liked three-year-old Ali better; she spoke more than she cried and helped more than she destroyed.

The luggage loading wasn't going very well. Alex put her hands on her hips and sighed heavily. Dad attempted bungee cords to secure the bags to the camper. Alex wondered how they would stay put rolling down the highway at high speed. Dad tried to show her how bungee cords worked, but every time he tried, he failed. He never did convince Alex that the luggage was safely secured to the camper.

Ali obviously disagreed. She stood back with her hands over her head and cheered for dad, who was her absolute hero. She clapped loudly and yelled, "Yay for daddy! Yay for daddy!", while Mom and Ali's older brother, Adam, walked out of the house carrying more bags.

Alex looked over when she heard the door slam behind them, and so did Ali. This time she put her hands out in front of her, palms facing out.

"No, no, no, no, no more bags!" Ali cried. "Daddy car FULL!"

"Well, too bad, shorty," Adam told his littlest sister, "I have more stuff to bring also." He walked past her toward the camper. Adam pulled the door open, disappeared inside, and wasn't seen again until the family was in motion.

Ali looked up at her mother with tears in her eyes. She put fists on her cheeks. She could be bossy but became very sad when people ignored her.

"He didn't listen! Daddy has no more room! I told him no more bags!" Ali started to cry. Her hands balled up into little fists that she put on each cheek as if to stop herself, but that never worked. Mom put down her bags and scooped her up. She whispered something soothing, as Mom always did. And Ali quickly stopped crying.

"...so, are we going to have fun?" Mom asked Ali in an exaggerated tone.

"YEAH!" Ali called. "Hooray!" Ali squirmed down, opened her hands, and ran back to dad.

Alex took all this in and sighed. *Here we go*, she thought, *another family road trip*. Alex picked up her backpack and slung it across her shoulder. She walked the camper length and saw her dad struggling with a knot of bungee cords. He was feverishly trying to dislodge the knot, but it was only getting worse from Alex's perspective. Like Ali, she glanced at the bags perched on top of the camper and wondered how they would stay in place once they started moving. Alex shrugged and moved on.

When she came to the door, she climbed the steps, entered, and closed her eyes. The familiar woodsy smell greeted her, and she couldn't help but remember years of beautiful memories of family trips. The Grand Canyon. The Great Lakes. Yellowstone National Park.

Alex opened her eyes. This year was going to be different. She and her family weren't going anywhere famous or exciting. "Staying local" is how her mother put it, and "saving on gas" is what her father said. They'd found a lovely campground about an hour from home, and they were heading there for a long weekend.

Pepper, the black lab, ran out of the house, barking her head off. Pepper loved camping. Alex's family brought her everywhere with them, and she loved the adventure. Paper enjoyed the hiking and exploring that went along with camping. She slept in the back next to her parent's bed. They shared that bed with Ali, while Adam and Alex each had a bunk. It was a snug fit, but it was fun. Usually.

An hour later, the Alloran family was on the road. Dad was in the driver's seat, and Mom was the navigator. She controlled the radio and called out driving directions. When someone needed a bathroom break, Mom found a stop - fast. Adam had music blaring into his head in no time, and Ali had already curled up on the bed and fallen fast asleep. Pepper was snoring quietly next to her. Alex sat with her head in her hand, watching the scenery fly.

Dad steered the camper expertly down the highway. All was well. Until Alex heard a weird *thump-dee-dump* from the roof of the camper, followed quickly by a few more bangs.

"What was that?" Dad asked nervously.

"I don't know," Mom said, "I'm going to look out the back." She unbuckled her seatbelt as Dad put on his hazard lights and steered onto the shoulder of the highway.

Alex watched Mom walk through the camper's kitchen and into her small bedroom. She lifted the curtain to the tiny window.

"OH, NO!" She called, waking both Ali and Pepper. Ali rubbed her eyes and repeated, "Oh no, oh no, oh no, oh no. Mama?"

Mom motioned for dad to come back and look also. Adam was oblivious to the fact that the camper had stopped. He was still bopping to the music pumping into his brain. Alex rolled her eyes at him and turned back to her parents, who were now alternating between looking out the window and looking at each other.

"What?" Alex asked, getting up from the little dinette. "What's going on?"

Her parents moved out of the way and Alex could see the stretch of the empty highway behind the camper. It was dotted with... suitcases?

The suitcases and duffel bags had not only come loose from the camper but most of them had also opened. Clothes blew out of the open bags and flew down the highway. Yellow tops, blue shorts, green belts, white sneakers, and red jackets all tumbled together in a living piece of art.

Alex started to laugh.

Pepper started to bark.

Adam pulled his earbuds out and turned around. "Why are we stopped?" He asked, crossly. He stood up from his bunk and joined the rest of the family, now all gathered around the tiny window.

"WHAT?" Adam screamed as he saw a multicolored pair of boxer shorts cross the highway median and start blowing off the side of the road. "Where are the rest of my clothes?!"

Adam had both of his hands on his head now, eyes bulging. Ali was giggling and holding her teddy bear; as long as she had her teddy bear, all was well.

"What now?" Mom asked Dad.

Dad scratched his head. "Well, he answered, "it would be too dangerous to go after them." Four cars whizzed by their camper as they spoke. "We can get through four days with what we are wearing, right?"

"WHAT!" Alex yelled. "Ew…, Dad, that's disgusting!"

A tractor-trailer sped by. Dad looked at Alex as if to say, "point made."

"Ugh!" Alex turned and went back to the dinette and buckled back in. Adam returned to his bunk with a grunted "whatever" under his breath.

Mom and dad shrugged at each other and slowly made their way back to the front. Dad buckled in. Mom sat for a moment, looking like she wanted to say something, but instead grabbed her seatbelt and said, "let's just go." She put her hands over her face and rubbed her eyes.

Alex thought - *this is not a good start.*

A few more miles down the highway, when Alex was deep into her book, there was a loud *POP* and the camper swerved left, then right, then left again, until dad slowly steered the camper once again to the shoulder. He turned the hazard lights on again and let out a loud sigh.

Mom put her hand on his shoulder. "You stay," she told him. She unbuckled her seatbelt, "I'll go."

Mom stood, stretched, and walked to the door. She opened the door and walked outside. The camper was silent and still. Mom returned in under a minute.

Dad unbuckled his seatbelt and stood up. "Well? What did you see?"

Mom looked at her feet and put her hands on her hips and smiled. Then she laughed. She lifted her head and stared at the ceiling of the camper and laughed as loudly as Alex had ever heard.

"Flat tire," Mom said, "we have a flat tire."

Dad sat down hard in the driver's seat and put his head down on the steering wheel. Ali started to cry and hugged her bear tighter, while Pepper walked to Ali and nuzzled her hand. Mom continued to laugh.

Adam once again looked up and said, "Now what?"

"We have a flat tire," Alex answered. For no reason at all, she repeated loudly, "Flat tire."

"I heard you the first time, brat," Adam shot back, "now what?"

"You don't have to be a jerk, jerk!" Alex shouted.

"Hey, hey!" Dad walked between them. "Enough. Let's work on the problem. We have a flat tire. It needs to get changed," dad thought for a moment, "Adam, you're with me."

Adam got up from his bunk and followed his father outside, obviously grumpy. Then the door slammed behind them, and the camper was silent again.

Ali uttered one word. "Hungry."

Mom and Alex's heads snapped up and looked at Ali. She repeated it, but it came out like a command this time.

"Hungry!"

"Of course," Mom said. "Alex, would you go into the snack cabinet and get Ali a bag of Snak-A-Dooz? She was rubbing her eyes again.

"Mom, do you have a headache?" Alex asked, heading to the snack cabinet.

"Yeah, honey, I do," Mom answered. She started rummaging through her pocket for painkillers.

Alex opened the food to the snack cabinet and reached in.

There was nothing.

"Uhm, Mom?"

Her mother had gone back up to her seat, where she had a can of soda to wash down her painkillers.

"Mom? Mom?" Alex called again. She saw her mother swallow hard and knew she'd finally got her painkillers down.

"What is it, honey?" Mom answered, looking tired and weak. Outside, Alex could hear dad and Adam starting to change the camper tire.

"The snack cabinet is empty."

"*Empty?*" Mom froze.

Alex nodded. She looked inside to be sure. She stuck her hand in and waved it around. "It's empty, mom."

Ali toddled over with Pepper behind her. She stuck her head inside the empty cabinet, and then stood up with tears in her eyes.

"No snack for Ali?" She said quietly. "No snacks?"

Mom looked at Alex. Alex shrugged.

"Oh no. Did Dad....?" Mom bolted outside the camper and Alex could hear their voices. They were muffled. Alex and Ali looked at each other.

"Don't worry, Ali," Alex said to her sister, "we'll get you snacks."

Mom was speaking loudly now, and she sounded annoyed. Dad sounded apologetic. Then the clanking and squeaking of a changing tire started again.

Mom came back up the camper steps and opened the door. She looked frustrated and defeated.

"The snacks were bungeed to the top of the camper," Mom told Alex and Ali. "Now they are" - she pointed down the back of the camper, where the tiny bedroom window was - "all over the highway, back there."

Ali walked to her mother and put her arms up to be held. Mom picked her up and cuddled her while she cried.

Adam and dad came back into the camper then, greasy and sweaty.

Adam asked how far we were from home.

"About an hour. What else could go wrong?" Dad answered.

Just then Ali looked up, and screamed, "Snacks on ROAD!!!"

"Huh?" Dad asked, confused.

Alex spoke up. "You tried to bungee cord the snack bag to the roof, instead of actually putting the snacks in the camper for the trip, and now they are all over the highway. Ali is hungry. And crying."

"Thank you, Alex," dad said, "I can hear her."

For a moment they all stood around in silence, except for Ali sobbing.

Mom broke the silence. "What town are we in?"

Dad looked out the window and looked up at a highway sign. He told everyone, "We are at Exit 13 in Tyson. Why?"

"Three more towns and there is a gigantic – MALL," Mom said as if a mall was where she wanted to be all along.

"New clothes," Alex said.

"A decent place to wash the grease off these hands!" Dad added.

"And snacks for Ali!" Ali clapped her hands.

Adam smiled. "Sounds like a plan."

Mom said, "OK! New road trip! Everyone, buckle up!"

THE TEXTING BABYSITTERS

Stacy
online

Hey A, wat r u doin 2nite?

Stacy - 6:05 p.m.

(...) (...)

Stacy - 6:07 p.m.

Hi Stace—got a call.
Yeah, old people still like, call doing.
I M bbystting, how bout u?

Amber - 6:22 p.m.

Me, 2. Who called?

Stacy - 6:24 p.m.

Message...

The Wilsons. Eva is their kid. Nice. Easy. I think Eva is 8? 9? Start @7:30.

Amber - 6:25 p.m.

Same here. @7. Tommy O'Hurley. He is 8, also??

Stacy - 6:26 p.m.

I babysat him last week. He has a snake!!!!!!!!

Amber - 6:26 p.m.

!!!!!SNAKE?!!!!!

Stacy - 6:26 p.m.

Message...

LOL yup OMG it is huuuuuuuge.

Amber - 6:27 p.m.

NONONONONONO. Ur kidding, RT?

Stacy - 6:27 p.m.

Nope. NOT kidding. Good luck

Amber - 6:28 p.m.

(...)

Stacy - 6:28 p.m.

Message...

128

(...)

Stacy - 6:29 p.m.

Sta? R U ok? R U there?

Amber - 6:30 p.m.

Mom is calling me 4 dinner. Gotta run.
Food and then leaving for SNAKEBOY. LOL.
Txt u l8r

Stacy - 6:30 p.m.

Byyyyyyyeeeeee

Amber - 6:30 p.m.

Message...

AMBER!!! U R a JOKER.

Stacy - 7:04 p.m.

AMBER. That snake is not huuuuuuge.

Stacy - 7:15 p.m.

A, the snake is little. And cuuuuuute.
His name is ELMO!!
Y did u tell me it wuz huuuuge?!

Stacy - 7:17 p.m.

Amber? R U getting theeeeez?

Stacy - 7:18 p.m.

Message...

130

(...)

Stacy - 7:19 p.m.

GOT YA!!!!

Amber - 7:34 p.m.

That was not nice, Amber.
I was really scared!
OMG I almost canceled!
But the snake is actually really cute.
Did u hold it when u were here?

Stacy - 7:35 p.m.

Ew, NO WAY. A slimy, slithery snake?
No chance.

Amber - 7:35 p.m.

Message...

LOL that's funny.
OK gotta get this kid into a bathtub.
Talk l8r.

Stacy - 7:36 p.m.

Byyyyyyeeeee!!!!!!

Amber - 7:36 p.m.

OMG Ambs, Tommy flooded the bathroom!
Water EVERYwhere! What a MESS!!!!!!!

Stacy - 8:05 p.m.

BWAHAHAHAHAHAHAHA!!!

Amber - 8:05 p.m.

Message...

Stacy
online

How is your night going?

Easy. Chicken nuggets into the toaster
Watched a little TV.
Eva is getting changed for bed.
She is brushing her teeth.

Amber - 8:06 p.m.

I don't hear the water.

Amber - 8:07 p.m.

I DO NOT HEAR THE WATER!

Amber - 8:08 p.m.

Message...

Stacy
online

Go find her!

Stacy - 8:09 p.m.

(...) (...) (...)

Amber - 8:09 p.m.

Amber? Did you find her?

Stacy - 8:13 p.m.

Amber?
Amber?
Amber?

Stacy - 8:14 p.m.

Message...

What's going on????????

Stacy - 8:15 p.m.

Stacy, have you ever lost a kid
when you were babysitting?????

Amber - 8:25 p.m.

OMG, Amber r u serious right now?????
Where have you looked????

Stacy - 8:26 p.m.

The entire house.
Bathroom
Bedroom
Kitchen
Den
Dining Room
Basement
Where else should I look?????????

Amber - 8:26 p.m.

Message...

(...)

Stacy - 8:27 p.m.

Stacy?

Amber - 8:28 p.m.

Stacy?

Amber - 8:28 p.m.

STACY!!!! WHERE ELSE SHOULD I LOOK??!!!!!!

Amber - 8:29 p.m.

Uh, now I have a problem here....

Stacy - 8:30 p.m.

136

Stacy
online

Can't B worse than losing a kid

Amber - 8:31 p.m.

Well......the snake got out.

Stacy - 8:31 p.m.

WHAT? WHAT? WHAT?

Amber - 8:31 p.m.

You lost a whole KID, Amber. I only lost a snake!

Stacy - 8:32 p.m.

WHAT DO WE DO?

Amber - 8:33 p.m.

Message...

137

STAY CALM. Let me think.
Tommy is calling me. I will txt when I can.

Stacy - 8:33 p.m.

Checking in. Update?

Amber - 8:50 p.m.

Nothing to report.
We took flashlights and searched the house.
Now I wish the snake was BIG!
Would be easier to find!!!!!
Tommy is asking to search the backyard.
I think his window is open....
Can snakes climb out a window?

Stacy - 8:52 p.m.

NO IDEA.
Still no little Eva here!
Funny, her window is open too...
(...) (...) (...)
Does Tommy live on 3rd St??

Amber - 8:53 p.m.

Message...

How did you know?
And WHY???

Stacy - 8:55 p.m.

OMG Stacy!
The kids are both 8, same grade.
Live on the same street.
Probably know each other.
Does Tommy have a tablet or phone?

Amber - 8:55 p.m.

YES!!! This is crazy!
His tablet is on his bed.
It's open.
Texting app.
Reading......
(...)

Stacy - 8:56 p.m.

Did he text Eva???

Amber - 8:56 p.m.

Message...

(...) (...) (...)

Stacy - 8:57 p.m.

WHAT DOES IT SAY???

Amber - 8:58 p.m.

He texted Eva alright.
Told her he took Elmo out of his cage
before his bath
And didn't put the top on right
And now the snake is gone.

Stacy - 8:58 p.m.

OMG.
Did Eva reply?

Amber - 9:00 p.m.

Message...

YUP.
She said "Coming over, gotta sneak out"

Stacy - 9:00 p.m.

!!!!!!!!!!!!!!!
She snuck out the window?
Where is Tommy now?

Amber - 9:01 p.m.

In the backyard with a flashlight
Looking for Elmo
WAIT
I C 2 LITES outside!!!

Stacy - 9:01 p.m.

Is Eva in the backyard?

Amber - 9:03 p.m.

Message...

Looking out the window
(...)
...at two little kids with lites walking around the backyard!!
I'm going out there.

Stacy - 9:03 p.m.

Walking over. House #?

Amber - 9:04 p.m.

19.

Stacy - 9:04 p.m.

I am at 25!! I knew this street looked familiar! I will be right there!

Amber - 9:05 p.m.

WAIT WAIT WAIT they are coming in

Stacy - 9:05 p.m.

Message...

Stacy
online

OK. Fill me in SOON

Amber - 9:06 p.m.

Stacy?

Amber - 9:07 p.m.

STACY?

Amber - 9:09 p.m.

STACY!!!
Eva's parents will be home soon!
What is happening?!?!?!?!?!?

Amber - 9:11 p.m.

Message...

143

OK OK OK
We have Elmo
We have Eva
We have Tommy
And now there is a LEAK from
the bathroom flood!

Stacy - 9:11 p.m.

LOLOLOLOL
Drip drip drip

Amber - 9:12 p.m.

NOT FUNNY
BIG MESS!
Come get Eva...
AND BRING TOWELS!

Stacy - 9:12 p.m.

Message...

144

CONCLUSION

So, you've finished the *Third Grade Book*. Congratulations!

You read about historical figures, what your pet may be thinking and doing when you go to school, and what a chance encounter with a celebrity might be like.

You read that heroes are not always grown-ups - they can save their friends or their farm!

What do you think makes a good story? Do you enjoy character descriptions or inanimate objects who can think for themselves?

Let's think about the people we met in this book.

If we had paired Maggie, the great best friend and basketball player from "She Shoots, She Scores!" with Carter on his farm, do you think his day would have been better? Why or why not?

If you remember "A Day in The Life of Pets," each animal had a distinctly different personality. Kala seemed to be the leader of the group, yet Hoover knew how to cross the street safely, and helped his friends each time they came to a busy corner.

And while cats and dogs seem more connected emotionally to their owners, it was Goldie who first mentioned missing Henry.

After reading this story, do you wonder what your pets, or any animals, are thinking about? Do you wonder if they can form friendships themselves?

Ask yourself a few of these questions:

- If I could be any of these characters, who would I be and why?
- If I were one of the Texting Babysitters, how could I have kept a better eye on the kids - and the snake?!
- Why was it important that Grandma remembered meeting Ruby Bridges (a true historical figure in American history), and that she told the story to her granddaughter?

I hope you enjoyed reading *Third Grade Book* as much as I enjoyed writing it. Never stop reading, or dreaming.

Made in the USA
Coppell, TX
10 October 2023

22620810R00085